Kiely

MACMILLAN **Very First DICTIONARY**

MACMILLAN Very First DICTIONARY

A *Magic World* of Words

Previously published as the *Macmillan Magic World of Words*.

Macmillan Publishing Company
New York

Collier Macmillan Publishers
London

The dictionary section of this book was previously published as the *Macmillan Magic World of Words*. For the book's reissue as the *Macmillan Very First Dictionary*, special sections on language and on the earth have been added. The sections on language, "How Words Came to Be" and "How Writing Came to Be," begin on page vi. The section on the earth, "Our Wonderful World," begins on page 257.

Staff

Editorial Director: William D. Halsey

Art Director: Zelda Haber

Artists: Dora Leder
Angela Adams
John Hamberger
Mordecai Gerstein
George Bakacs

Definers: Phyllis R. Winant
Vesta K. Wells

Assistant Art Director: Trudy Veit

Educational Consultant: Sandra Maccarone

Library of Congress Catalog Card Number 82-22901   ISBN 0-02-761730-0

Macmillan Publishing Company, 866 Third Avenue, New York, New York 10022
Collier Macmillan Canada, Inc.

Manufactured in the United States of America
10 9 8 7 6

How to Help a Child Use This Book

The *Macmillan Very First Dictionary* is an alphabetical wordbook that introduces a child to dictionary skills. It is designed for those children who have progressed beyond the very simple *Macmillan Picture Wordbook,* but are not yet ready to use a full-fledged dictionary, such as the *Macmillan Dictionary for Children*. This book consists of an alphabetical list of the most common words of the English language. Each word is accompanied by an explanation of its meaning. The explanation consists of a series of sentences that define the word and show how it is used in context. Nearly 1,500 words are explained in all.

The *Macmillan Very First Dictionary* contains almost 500 illustrations created especially for this book. A unique feature of the book is that these illustrations are used exclusively to explain conceptual words that express ideas, rather than words that describe things. Words such as *alike, single, hurry,* and *empty* are illustrated, while words such as *airplane, horse,* and *dish* are not. The reason for this is that these conceptual words are the ones that young children have the most difficulty in understanding, and that adults have the most difficulty in explaining.

In the *Macmillan Very First Dictionary,* definitions are phrased like an adult's answers to a child's questions—they read as if the child had just asked "What does _____ mean?" or "What's a _____?" ("An **alarm** is a thing that makes a loud noise ..." and so forth.) Also, example sentences are written within the context of a child's experience—they deal with parents, brothers, sisters, grandparents, friends, school, and so on.

This book is intended to serve children at different age levels. The youngest child can learn his or her *ABC*'s from the special pages that introduce each letter of the alphabet. A child who is ready to read, or just learning, can move from the alphabet page into the body of the text by finding the words that go with the pictures on the same page, and can also learn to identify and understand the entry words that are illustrated on each page by relating each one to the appropriate picture. A child who has learned to read can easily use the *Macmillan Very First Dictionary* alone, because of the book's simple format and low reading level.

The purpose of the *Macmillan Very First Dictionary* is to help children learn about words. We hope that you and the child or children to whom you are giving this book will find it enjoyable and rewarding.

—The Editors

v

How Words Came to Be

Many, many years ago, people did not know how to talk. These early people pointed their fingers or waved their arms to give messages. They probably made some sounds, like "mm" or "huh" or "ugh." But they did not have words.

Then, after thousands of years had passed, the early people began to use words. Perhaps one person said "water" when he or she was thirsty and other people began to say "water," too. No one knows for sure.

We don't know just what words were used first or when they came into use. But a few of the words we use today can be traced to easy baby sounds.

A baby says "ma ma ma" and "da da da." Who are the first people the baby knows? For most babies, they are Mama and Dada. And the words for those people in some languages are like these easy baby sounds.

Some other words are like sounds we hear around us. We say bees *buzz*. Buzz is a word like the sound that bees make. We say dogs *bark*. Bark sounds like the sound a dog makes. We say a big bell goes *ding-dong*. These words are like the sounds themselves. Can you think of others?

WATER

WATER

BUZZ

BARK

RIBIT

When we are young, we learn words by hearing other people say them. We learn words like *sleep, eat, no!* and *I love you.* Later we learn to read and write. We learn more words as we read them.

For a long time, early people did not know how to read or write. They learned all their words by hearing them. As the early people moved from place to place, they sometimes changed the sound of a word a little. So we say "mama" or "mother" in English. A German child says *"Mutter."* A Russian child says *"mati."* A child who speaks Spanish says *"madre."* Long ago these words all came from the same word. We say they come from the same *root* word. And they have the same meaning.

The words we speak are in the English language. English has words from many other languages. And many other languages have some words from the same roots as ours. The word *milk* is an example. Its root is *meolc.* In other languages today the word for milk is *milch* or *melk.* These words come from the same root word as milk.

Not all languages have the same root word for milk. In French, the word for milk is *lait.* It sounds like "lay." In Spanish, milk is *leche.* In Italian, it is *latte.* These words come from the root word *lac.*

Today people speak more than 3,000 different languages in different parts of the world. In some lands, people who live just a few miles from one another speak different languages. They use different words for the same things. They cannot understand one another. This makes it hard to be friends.

If someone said to you, *"Apportez-moi du lait, s'il vous plaît,"* would you understand? Not unless you knew the French language. Would you understand *"Traigame leche, por favor"*? Not unless you knew a little Spanish. Those sentences sound very different from "Bring me some milk, please," in English. But they mean the same thing.

Sometimes a word gets a new meaning in the same language. Take our word *car.* To us a car means an automobile. But the word *car* used to have another meaning. Long, long ago, people used a cart that they called a *carrus.* As many years went by, the word *carrus* became *cart* or *car.* These carts or cars were very useful.

They were made in many lands. Words for them—*car, carro, carre, kara*—came into many languages.

Later there were *railway cars* and *streetcars.* Then the automobile was invented. Many English-speaking people called it a *car.* So the old word came to stand for something new.

Not all languages use the same word for car. In French the word is *voiture.* In Spanish it is *coche* or *carro.* In German the word for car is *Wagen.*

Sometimes a new word is needed. *Carport* is quite a new word. Some people keep a car in a carport. The word *port* means a harbor or other safe place for a ship. So the word *car* added to the word *port* means a safe place or shelter for a car.

That is the way new words come to be. When we have something new we need a word for, we often make the new word from old roots. Our language is growing with new words all the time.

How Writing

People learned how to talk many years before they learned how to write. Without writing, they could not send a message to a friend who was far away. They could not keep a record of things they sold or traded.

Then, about 5,000 years ago, people started to draw pictures that told messages. That was the first way of writing, called *picture writing.* At first people just drew pictures of things—a deer, a man or woman, a boat, a house, a fire.

Later they drew pictures for other words like *travel, give, pay, love.* Then they could send long messages. They could keep count of what they sold or traded. They did all this with small pictures and lines.

Came to Be

The old land of Egypt had beautiful picture writing. Some of it was carved in stone. The carving took a long time, but it has lasted for thousands of years. We can still see some of this picture writing today.

As time passed, picture writing came to have more and more words. The people in Egypt could write longer and longer messages. They could write poems. They could even write books. They wrote their books on long pieces of paper called *papyrus* that they could unroll and roll up. They did not turn pages as we do today.

In China long ago, people used a different picture for every word they wrote. It took them a long time to draw all these pictures. So they changed many of the pictures to a few quick lines and boxes. These simplified pictures were called *characters*. (Writing with characters is still used in China to this day.)

People used picture writing for many, many years. Then after a long time someone thought of using simple signs for each sound in a word. We call the sign that stands for a sound a *letter*. All the letters we use make up the *alphabet*. Not all languages use the same alphabet. But most languages today use some kind of alphabet.

The letters in our English alphabet look quite different from the letters in some other alphabets. And some alphabets use more letters than we use in English. The

Russian language has 33 letters in its alphabet. Some languages have even more. Do you know how many letters the English alphabet has? The right answer is 26.

We put our 26 letters together to make thousands and thousands of words. There are so many English words! You can learn a new word every day as long as you live. You will never know them all. But it is fun to know and use new words. You will find nearly 1,500 in this book.

How to Use Your Book

The *Macmillan Very First Dictionary* is *your* book. We hope that it will teach you all about words. But before you really get into the book, we'd like to tell you a few things about it. You can learn much more from your book if you know how it works.

There are four easy steps that you can follow to use this book. For example, let's suppose you wanted to know about a certain word— *center*. This is how you would use your book to learn what *center* means.

LOVE

HUG

PARTY

CUTE

COMFORTABLE

NAP

Step 1: The *Macmillan Very First Dictionary* is a long list of words. These words are put in the book in the same *ABC* order as the letters of the alphabet. All the words that begin with *A* come first, then the words that begin with *B,* then *C,* and so on. To find the word *center,* the first thing you have to do is find the page with the big letter *C.* Because *C* is one of the first letters, the *C* page is near the front of the book. It's page 34.

Step 2: Now that you have found the page for the letter *C,* you can see that it is followed by all the words that begin with *C.* These words are also in *ABC* order—*CA* words come first, and so on. If you look through the *C* pages, you will find *center* on page 40.

Step 3: To make it easier to find, your word is printed in heavy black letters like this—**center.** Under the word you will find what is called a definition. The definition tells what the word means— "A center is a place that is in the middle of something." After the definition comes something else that tells you about the word. This is called the example sentence. It shows you how the word is used: "Mom put the plate of cookies in the **center** of the table."

Step 4: After the example sentence, there is a special sign like this ☼ and the words *"See the picture."* This tells you to look for a picture of the word *center.* The picture is at the top of the page, and the example sentence appears again under it. If you look at the example sentence, you will see that it tells you what is going on in the picture. The words and the picture go together.

That's really all you have to know to begin to use this book. We hope you will learn a lot from it.

PULL

KIND

apple   See page 10

alligator   See page 5

ape   See page 10

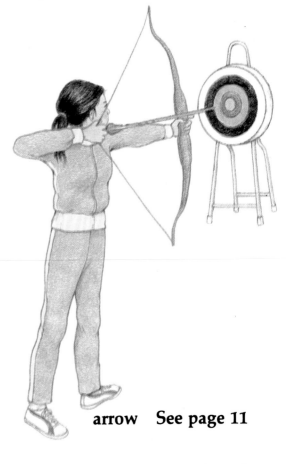

arrow   See page 11

On this page are pictures of words that begin with the letter "A". Can you find each word in your book? Turn to the page number you see near the picture. When you find the right word you will see this: ■

a

I have **a** pet cat. The mailman comes to our house once **a** day. The rose is **a** flower.

able

When you are **able** to do something, it means that you know how to do it. Harry is **able** to count up to twenty. Mary is **able** to ride her new bicycle.

about

My sister is reading a book **about** horses. The airplane was **about** to take off. There are **about** twenty boys and girls in my class at school.

above

The birds flew **above** the trees. The sun is shining **above.**

absent

When you are **absent,** you are away from a place. Sally is **absent** from school today because she is sick.

accident

An **accident** is something that happens. Some **accidents** are bad. Mary had an **accident** while she was roller-skating and fell down. ☼*See the picture.* Terry found a dime by **accident** while she was looking for her shoes under the bed.

ache

Ache means that something hurts. Bob's arm **ached** after he pitched the whole baseball game.

Mary had an **accident** while she was roller-skating and fell down.

1

Bobby sailed his toy airplane **across** the pond.

across
Bobby sailed his toy airplane **across** the pond.
☀️*See the picture.* We walked **across** the street.

act
Act means to do something. The firemen **acted** quickly to put out the fire. George is **acting** the part of an Indian in our Thanksgiving play.

add
Add means to put things together. If you **added** the numbers 5 and 4, you would get 9. Ellen likes **adding** lots of sugar to her cereal.

address
An **address** is the place where you live. Carol's **address** is 34 James Street.

adult

An **adult** is a person who is grown-up. Your mother and father are **adults.** My teacher is an **adult.**

advertisement

An **advertisement** is something that tells about a thing you can buy. There were many **advertisements** in the newspaper about cars for sale.

afraid

When you are **afraid,** it means you are scared of something. Our dog was **afraid** of the storm and hid in his doghouse. ☼*See the picture.*

Our dog was **afraid** of the storm and hid in his doghouse.

after

Nancy ran **after** the ball. Dan came to my house **after** school yesterday. Tuesday comes **after** Monday.

afternoon

Afternoon is a time of day. It is the part of the day between noon and evening. We have play time at school in the **afternoon.**

again

When you do something **again,** you do it one more time. Diane called her dog and when he didn't come, she called him **again.**

against

Tom threw the ball **against** the wall. ☼*See the picture.* Our school played a baseball game **against** another school.

Tom threw the ball **against** the wall.

age

Age is how old you are. My sister's **age** is five years.

ago

Ago means before the time it is now. The movie started a few minutes **ago.**

agree

When you **agree** with people, you think the same way that they do. Karen thought it would be fun to go on a picnic, and Fred **agreed.**

ahead

Peggy was **ahead** of the others in the race. ☼*See the picture.* Our team was two points **ahead** in the game.

Peggy was **ahead** of the others in the race.

air

Air is what we breathe. **Air** is all around us. Mary blew **air** into her balloon.

airplane

An **airplane** is a thing that can fly in the air. It has two wings and an engine to make it go. An **airport** is a place where **airplanes** land.

alarm

An **alarm** is a thing that makes a loud noise. The **alarm** of a clock wakes people up in the morning. The fire **alarm** in the building tells people that there is danger.

All the puppies look very much **alike.**

alike

When things are **alike,** it means they are almost the same. All the puppies look very much **alike.** ☼*See the picture.* Betsy and her sister sometimes dress **alike.**

alive

When something is **alive,** it means it is living. You are **alive.** Harry has to water the flowers if he wants to keep them **alive.**

all

Dick ate **all** the cookies in the box. **All** of us are going to go swimming this afternoon.

alligator

An **alligator** is an animal. It has a long tail and short legs and a large mouth. **Alligators** live in rivers. ■

almost

Lewis is **almost** as tall as his father. ☼*See the picture.* I am **almost** finished with my homework.

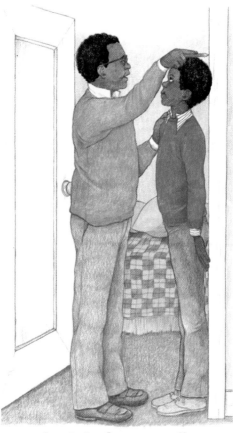

Lewis is **almost** as tall as his father.

alone

If you are **alone** you are not with anyone. There was just one kitten all **alone** in the window of the pet store.

along

People stood all **along** the street as the parade passed by. Ruth brought **along** a ball to the park.

alphabet

The **alphabet** is the letters we use to write words. The letters of the **alphabet** go in a special way. "A" is the first letter of the **alphabet.**

already

My sister has finished her homework **already.** You are **already** late for school.

also

Chris is wearing a blue coat and his sister is wearing one **also.** ☼*See the picture.*

Chris is wearing a blue coat and his sister is wearing one **also.**

always
If something **always** happens it means that it happens all the time. My dog **always** barks when he sees me coming.

am
I **am** happy that you can come over to play.

amaze
When something is **amazing,** it surprises you very much. The children were **amazed** by the magic tricks. ☼*See the picture.*

ambulance
An **ambulance** is a special kind of car. **Ambulances** are used to carry hurt or sick people to a hospital.

The children were **amazed** by the magic tricks.

American
If something is **American** it means that it belongs to the United States. Someone who lives in the United States is called an **American.**

among
Nan divided the cake **among** her friends. There was one black rabbit **among** the white rabbits. ☼*See the picture.*

amuse
Amuse means to make someone happy. When something is **amusing,** it makes you smile or laugh. The clowns **amused** everyone with their silly way of walking.

There was one black rabbit **among** the white rabbits.

7

an

A bear is **an** animal. Tom ate **an** orange. We saw **an** elephant at the zoo.

and

Betty has a dog **and** a cat. Sally **and** Tim played ball with me.

angry

When you are **angry,** you feel very mad. Matt was **angry** because his little brother broke his toy truck. ☼*See the picture.*

animal

An **animal** is any living thing that is not a plant. A boy, a girl, a cow, a bird, a fish, a snake, a mosquito, and a worm are all **animals.**

ankle

The **ankle** is a part of your body. Your **ankles** are between your feet and your legs.

answer

Answer means to say something when someone asks you a question or calls you. Amy **answered** the teacher's question. Mother called Barbara three times, but she didn't **answer.** Dick **answered** the telephone. Alice didn't know the **answers** to her father's questions.

another

Do you want **another** cookie? Joan ate her hot dog and then asked for **another.**

ant

An **ant** is a small insect. **Ants** live in the ground.

Matt was **angry** because his little brother broke his toy truck.

any

Karen can swim faster than **any** of her friends. The cat doesn't have **any** food on his plate. ☼*See the picture.*

anyone

Anyone can play on the swings in the playground. **Anybody** can go swimming in the town pool.

anything

Do you want **anything** to eat? Susan doesn't look **anything** like her sister.

apart

If you take something **apart,** you make it into pieces. Joe took his toy airplane **apart** to find out what was wrong with it. One sheep stood **apart** from the rest of the flock. ☼*See the picture.*

The cat doesn't have **any** food on his plate.

One sheep stood **apart** from the rest of the flock.

9

apartment

An **apartment** is a place to live. Each of the **apartments** in that building has five rooms.

ape

An **ape** is a large animal that looks something like a person. **Apes** are like monkeys. ■

apologize

Apologize means to say you are sorry. You **apologize** when you have done or said something bad. Ellen **apologized** to her mother for breaking the glass.

Billy always has a big **appetite** after he plays football.

appetite

When you have an **appetite** you want to eat. Our dog had no **appetite** when she was sick. Billy always has a big **appetite** after he plays football. ☼*See the picture.*

apple

An **apple** is something to eat. It is a round fruit. **Apples** are red, yellow, or green. ■

are

We **are** going to the circus today. **Aren't** means "are not." **Aren't** they coming to the playground with us?

argue

Argue means to fight with words. When we **argue,** we talk in a loud, angry way. The boys playing baseball **argued** over whether the player was safe or out. ☼*See the picture.* Frank and his brother had an **argument** about whose turn it was to clean up their room.

arithmetic

When you use **arithmetic,** you use numbers to find the answer to a problem. You learn how to add, subtract, multiply, and divide when you study **arithmetic.**

arm

The **arm** is a part of your body. Your **arms** are between your shoulders and your wrists.

army

An **army** is a large group of people. An **army** fights for its country in a war.

around

Sue put her arms **around** her baby brother. ☼*See the picture.*

arrest

When the police **arrest** someone, they stop the person and hold him. The police **arrested** the man who tried to rob the store.

arrow

An **arrow** is a pointed stick. Indians used to hunt with **arrows** shot from a bow. The **arrow** on the sign points the way to the highway. ■

The boys playing baseball **argued** over whether the player was safe or out.

Sue put her arms **around** her baby brother.

art

Art is things that you make that are pretty. Paintings and drawings are **art.** The **artist** painted a picture of a boy and his dog.

as

Jan can swim **as** well **as** Mike can. Betty is in the same class **as** Tom.

ashamed

Ashamed means feeling sorry. When we are **ashamed,** we feel bad about something wrong or silly that we have done. Joan was **ashamed** of having yelled at her brother.

ask

When you **ask** a question, you want to know something. I **asked** Eric if he knew where my baseball was. Marcia always **asks** her mother for dessert when she finishes her dinner.

asleep

When you are **asleep,** you are not awake. Dad fell **asleep** in his chair after dinner. ☼*See the picture.*

Dad fell **asleep** in his chair after dinner.

at

The bird was **at** the top of the tree. I go to bed **at** eight o'clock. Joan looked **at** the pictures in the magazine.

ate

Bob **ate** two sandwiches for lunch yesterday.

attention

When you pay **attention,** you watch and listen carefully. The children paid **attention** to the teacher. ☼*See the picture.*

aunt

Your **aunt** is your father's or mother's sister. Your uncle's wife is also your **aunt.**

automobile

An **automobile** is something to ride in. **Automobiles** have four wheels and an engine to make them go. An **automobile** is the same thing as a **car.**

autumn

Autumn is a time of year. It comes between summer and winter. It is also called **fall.**

awake

When you are **awake** you are not sleeping. I was already **awake** when Mom called me.

away

I have to put my toys **away** before I go to bed. When the rabbit saw us he ran **away.**
☼*See the picture.*

The children paid **attention** to the teacher.

When the rabbit saw us he ran **away.**

13

bear   See page 19

banana   See page 16

Bb

broom   See page 30

bicycle   See page 23

On this page are pictures of words that begin with the letter "B". Can you find each word in your book? Turn to the page number you see near the picture. When you find the right word you will see this: ■

baby

A **baby** is a very young child. **Babies** do not know how to walk or talk.

baby-sitter

A **baby-sitter** is someone who takes care of you when your parents go out.

back

The **back** of something is the part that is behind the front. Johnny scratched his **back.** Sue threw the ball **back** to Jim.

backward

When something is going **backward,** it is going toward the back. Jerry wore his baseball cap **backward.** Greg looked **backward** to see if his dog was following him. ☼*See the picture.*

bacon

Bacon is something to eat. It is meat from a pig.

bad

When something is **bad,** it is not good. If you are being **bad,** it means that you are doing something wrong. Linda felt **bad** because she was mean to her friend. Mike has a **bad** cold. Our team played **badly,** and we lost the game.

bag

A **bag** is something used to hold things. Jerry ate a whole **bag** of candy. The man at the store put the food we bought into paper **bags.**

bake

Bake means to cook food in an oven. Jean **baked** cookies for the party. A **bakery** is a place where cookies and cakes are sold.

Greg looked **backward** to see if his dog was following him.

15

The seal **balanced** a ball on his nose.

balance

Balance means to keep in a place. The seal **balanced** a ball on his nose. ☼*See the picture.*

ball

A **ball** is something round. This **ball** is made of rubber. My kitten likes to play with **balls** of string. Jack threw the **ball** to Mary.

balloon

A **balloon** is a thing that you blow air into. It is made of rubber. **Balloons** get big when you fill them with air. Sarah's **balloon** broke when Don stuck a pin in it.

banana

A **banana** is something to eat. **Bananas** are long and have a yellow skin. A **banana** is a fruit. ■

band

A **band** is people that make music together. Do you know the name of the song that the **band** is playing? My brother plays the drums in the school **band.**

bandage

A **bandage** is a thing that is put over a cut. The doctor put **bandages** on Laura's cuts after she fell off her bicycle.

bank

A **bank** is a place to keep money. Dad went to the **bank** in town to take out some money. Jim put a nickel in his toy **bank.**

bar

A **bar** is a long piece of something. You use a **bar** of soap when you take a bath. Our parakeet's cage has **bars.**

barbecue

A **barbecue** is food cooked outdoors over a fire. Dad is going to **barbecue** hamburgers. ☼*See the picture.*

barber

A **barber** is someone who cuts your hair. Mom took me to the **barber** shop to have my hair cut.

bark

1. **Bark** is the skin of a tree. It is thick and rough.
2. **Bark** also means the sound that a dog makes. My dog **barks** when he wants his dinner.

Dad is going to **barbecue** hamburgers.

barn

A **barn** is a building on a farm. A farmer keeps his cows and horses in a **barn.**

baseball

Baseball is a game. It is played with a ball and a bat. The players try to hit the ball with the bat.

basket

A **basket** is something used to hold things. Mom keeps her sewing things in a **basket.** We bought two **baskets** of apples from the farmer.

basketball

Basketball is a game played with a large ball. The players try to throw the ball up in the air through a ring.

bat

1. A **bat** is a strong wooden stick. You use a **bat** to hit the ball in a baseball game.
2. A **bat** is also a small animal. It looks like a mouse with wings. **Bats** fly around at night.

bath

When you take a **bath,** you wash yourself. Sue takes a **bath** every night. Jim doesn't like to give his dog a **bath.** ☼*See the picture.*

bathing suit

A **bathing suit** is something to wear. We wear **bathing suits** when we go swimming.

bathroom

A **bathroom** is a room where you wash yourself. A **bathroom** has a sink where you wash your hands and brush your teeth. It also has a **bathtub** where you take a bath.

Jim doesn't like to give his dog a **bath**.

That horse will **be** a fast runner when he grows up.

be

Barbara is going to **be** six years old tomorrow. That horse will **be** a fast runner when he grows up. ☼*See the picture.*

beach

A **beach** is the land close to the water. **Beaches** are covered with sand. Nan likes to go to the **beach** and swim in the ocean.

bean

A **bean** is something to eat. It is a kind of seed. **Beans** are vegetables. Some **beans** that people eat are lima **beans** and string **beans.**

bear

A **bear** is a large animal. **Bears** have thick brown, black, or white fur. ■

beat

1. **Beat** means to hit something again and again. Joe was **beating** the drum loudly. ☼*See the picture.*
2. **Beat** also means that you do something better than someone else. Nancy was **beaten** by Ann in the running race.

Joe was **beating** the drum loudly.

19

beautiful

When something is **beautiful,** it is very pretty to look at. The Christmas tree was **beautiful** when its lights were on.

because

Because is a word you use when you tell why something is happening. The players were happy **because** they won the game.

become

Jean hopes to **become** a doctor when she grows up. The seed I planted will **become** a plant. Pat **became** tired after playing all day.

bed

A **bed** is a place to sleep. I go to **bed** at seven o'clock. Timmy has his own **bedroom.**

bee

A **bee** is an insect. It is black and yellow and has wings. **Bees** make honey.

been

Ted and Josh have **been** playing in the yard.

before

The bird flew away **before** the cat could catch it. ☼*See the picture.*

begin

When you **begin** to do something, you start to do it. Have you **begun** your homework yet? The sun was out, but later it **began** to rain.

behave

When you **behave,** it means that you are being good. The teacher told the children to **behave** in the classroom.

The bird flew away **before** the cat could catch it.

The baby chickens walked **behind** their mother.

behind
Carl sits **behind** Pete in school. The baby chickens walked **behind** their mother. ☼*See the picture.*

being
The baby is **being** washed. Two new houses are **being** built on our street.

believe
When you **believe** something, it means that you think it is true. Do you **believe** that story? My little sister **believes** in Santa Claus. Ted **believed** Alice when she said she was sorry.

bell
A **bell** is something that makes a ringing sound. I went to the door and rang the **bell.**

belong
When something **belongs** to you, it means that you own it. Does this ball **belong** to Ann or her brother? Mom said that the books **belonged** on the shelf, not on the floor.

below
Jerry hung one picture **below** the other. ☼*See the picture.*

Jerry hung one picture **below** the other.

21

belt

A **belt** is something to wear. You wear a **belt** around your waist.

bend

When you **bend** something, you move it so that it is not straight. If you **bend** your knees, your legs are not straight. Sam **bent** over to tie his shoes.

berry

A **berry** is something to eat. It is a small fruit. Strawberries and blackberries are **berries.**

The lions rested **beside** the river.

beside

Tim sits **beside** Dick at school. There is a tree **beside** our house. The lions rested **beside** the river. ☼*See the picture.*

best

I like chocolate ice cream **best.** Kate won the race because she is the **best** runner.

better

Nancy is a good swimmer, but Lucy is **better**.
Bob is feeling **better** today.

between

Karen stood **between** her mother and father.
The monkey put his tail **between** the bars.
☼*See the picture.*

The monkey put his tail **between** the bars.

Bible

The **Bible** is a book that tells about God. It
was written very long ago.

bicycle

A **bicycle** is a thing to ride on. **Bicycles** have
two wheels. A **bicycle** is also called a **bike.** ■

big

When something is **big,** it means that it is
large. Sharon has two **big** dogs. ☼*See the
picture.* Jerry wears a **bigger** coat than his baby
brother does. New York is the **biggest** city in
the United States.

bill

1. A **bill** is a piece of paper
that tells you how much you
must pay for something.
Mom paid the **bill** for the
groceries.
2. A **bill** is also a piece of
paper money. I have a dollar
bill.

bird

A **bird** is an animal with
wings. **Birds** can fly. They
are covered with feathers
and have two legs.

Sharon has two **big** dogs.

23

Christopher's friends came to his **birthday** party.

birthday

Your **birthday** is the day of the year you were born on. Christopher's friends came to his **birthday** party. ☼*See the picture.*

bite

Bite means to cut something with your teeth. Sandy **bit** into the apple. The dog has **bitten** a hole in my old shoe. The fish are not **biting** today. Harry has two mosquito **bites** on his leg.

black

Black is a very dark color. When you turn off all the lights in a room, the room is **black**.

blackboard

A **blackboard** is a thing to write on. Our teacher uses chalk to write on the **blackboard.**

blame

Blame means to say that a person has done something wrong. Mother **blamed** me for letting the bird out of its cage. Ann took the **blame** for breaking the window with the ball.

blanket

A **blanket** is something that keeps you warm. You put **blankets** on a bed.

bleed

When you **bleed,** blood comes out of your skin. Tom **bled** when he cut himself.

block

1. A **block** is a hard piece of something. Kim built a house with her wooden **blocks.**
2. A **block** is also a street. Helen and her friend live on the same **block.**

blood

Blood is the bright red liquid that comes out when you cut yourself. Your heart makes the **blood** go to all parts of your body.

blow

Blow means to make air go out of your mouth. We are going to **blow** up balloons for the party. The wind **blew** Ellen's hat off. ☼*See the picture.*

board

A **board** is a piece of wood. **Boards** are long and flat. They are used to build houses and other things.

The wind **blew** Ellen's hat off.

Tommy **boosted** his friend up the tree so that he could reach the apple.

boat

A **boat** is a thing that carries you over the water. Uncle Alex and Uncle Ted went fishing on the lake in their **boats.**

body

Your **body** is all of you. When you take a bath you wash your **body.** Elephants have very large **bodies.**

boil

Boil means to make water very hot. When water **boils,** little bubbles come to the top. Mother **boiled** eggs for the picnic.

bone

A **bone** is a part of your body. **Bones** are hard. Jack broke a **bone** in his arm when he fell out of the tree.

book

A **book** is something to read. **Books** have pages with writing and pictures on them. I am reading a **book** about a clown.

boost

Boost means to push up. Tommy **boosted** his friend up the tree so that he could reach the apple. ☼*See the picture.*

boot

A **boot** is something to wear on your foot. Debbie wears rubber **boots** when she plays in the snow.

born

When you are **born** it means that you begin living. My baby brother was **born** last month. The puppies were **born** yesterday.

26

borrow

Borrow means to take something for a while. May I **borrow** your roller skates? Mary **borrowed** a book from the library.

both

Both children won a prize. ☼*See the picture.*

bottle

A **bottle** is a thing used to hold something that you can pour. Mom bought two **bottles** of orange juice.

bottom

The **bottom** is the lowest part of something. Catherine was at the top of the slide, and her brother was at the **bottom**. ☼*See the picture.*

Both children won a prize.

Catherine was at the top of the slide, and her brother was at the **bottom**.

27

Lynn **bounced** the ball to her baby brother.

bounce

Bounce means to move up and down. Lynn **bounced** the ball to her baby brother. ☼*See the picture.*

bow

1. A **bow** is something that you tie. Carol tied the ribbons in her hair into **bows.**
2. A **bow** is also a thing to shoot arrows from. It is a thin piece of wood with a string tied to each end.

box

A **box** is something used to hold things. Phil put his toy trains in a **box.** Please hand me those two **boxes** of cereal.

boy

A **boy** is a child who will grow up to be a man. **Boys** are male children.

brain

Your **brain** is a part of your body. It is inside your head. Your **brain** is what you use to think and learn. Animals have **brains** too.

branch

A **branch** is a part of a tree. **Branches** grow out of the trunk of a tree. A bird built a nest on a **branch** of the tree in front of our house.

brave

If you are **brave,** it means that you are not afraid of anything. The **brave** girl climbed the big tree to bring down the kitten. ☼*See the picture.*

The **brave** girl climbed the big tree to bring down the kitten.

bread
Bread is something to eat. It is made of flour.

break
Break means to make something come to pieces. The glass will **break** if you drop it.

breakfast
Breakfast is food. You eat **breakfast** in the morning when you get up.

breath
Breath is the air you take in and let out when you **breathe.** You can **breathe** through your nose or your mouth.

bridge
A **bridge** is a road that crosses over something. We had to walk on a **bridge** to get to the other side of the river.

bright
When something is **bright,** it is very shiny. Sunlight made the room **bright.**

bring
Bring means to carry something to a place. Tom **brings** his lunch to school each day.

broke
The ball **broke** the window. ☼*See the picture.*

The ball **broke** the window.

broom
A **broom** is a brush with a long handle. It is used to clean the floor. ■

brother
Your **brother** is a boy who has the same mother and father as you.

brought

Everyone **brought** birthday presents for Tom to the party. My dog **brought** the newspaper to me. ☼*See the picture.*

brush

A **brush** is a thing to clean with. The parts of a **brush** pick up dirt. A toothbrush and a hairbrush are kinds of **brushes.** Mary **brushed** her hair to make it smooth. Jim **brushes** his dog every day.

bug

A **bug** is an insect. Ants and bees are **bugs.**

build

Build means to make something. Carl **built** a house with his blocks. The beaver was **building** a dam across the pond. ☼*See the picture.* Houses, schools, and churches are **buildings.**

My dog **brought** the newspaper to me.

The beaver was **building** a dam across the pond.

bulldozer

A **bulldozer** is a thing used to move rocks and dirt. It has an engine to make it go. The men used **bulldozers** to make the land flat for a road.

bullet

A **bullet** is a small piece of metal. **Bullets** are shot from guns.

bump

Bump means to knock into something. Sally **bumped** her knee on the chair. Johnny rode his bicycle over a **bump** in the road. ☼*See the picture.*

bunch

When you have a **bunch** of something, you have a lot of it. Vicky picked a **bunch** of flowers. Mom bought two **bunches** of grapes.

burn

Burn means to be on fire. We watched the logs **burn** in the fireplace. Jean **burnt** her finger on the hot iron.

bus

A **bus** is something to ride in. It has seats for many people. It is a kind of large car. My brother and I go to school on a **bus.**

bush

A **bush** is a small tree. Roses and berries grow on **bushes.**

business

Business is the work someone does to get money. My mother's and father's **business** is running a book store.

Johnny rode his bicycle over a **bump** in the road.

The bakery was very **busy** on Sunday.

busy

When you are **busy** you are doing something.
The bakery was very **busy** on Sunday. ☼*See the picture.*

but

Dick is tall, **but** his brother is taller.

button

A **button** is a small, round thing. The **buttons** on your clothes keep them closed.

buy

Buy means to get something by giving money for it. Sue is going to **buy** a new dress to wear to the party.

by

My dog likes to lie **by** the fire. ☼*See the picture.* The car went **by** us.

My dog likes to lie **by** the fire.   **33**

carrot   See page 38

clock   See page 46

camel   See page 36

On this page are pictures of words that begin with the letter "C". Can you find each word in your book? Turn to the page number you see near the picture. When you find the right word you will see this: ■

cab

A **cab** is a car. You pay the driver of a **cab** to take you someplace. A **cab** is the same as a **taxi.** My mother took a **cab** to the train station.

cafeteria

A **cafeteria** is a place to eat. In a **cafeteria,** you get the food and take it to a table to eat. Our school has a **cafeteria.**

cage

A **cage** is something to keep an animal in. It has bars or wire on the sides. The tigers at the zoo live in **cages.**

cake

A **cake** is something to eat. **Cakes** taste sweet. Jim's birthday **cake** had six candles on it.

calendar

A **calendar** is something that shows the days of the year. Ellen marked her birthday on the **calendar.**

calf

1. A **calf** is a baby cow.
2. The **calf** is also a part of your leg. Your **calves** are at the back of your legs between your knees and your ankles.

call

1. **Call** means to say something in a loud voice. Ben's dog always comes when he **calls** him. ☼*See the picture.*
2. **Call** also means to give a name to someone. Sandy **called** her new dog "King."

Ben's dog always comes when he **calls** him.

came

My father **came** to pick me up at school.

camel

A **camel** is an animal. It has a long neck and a big bump on its back. **Camels** live in the desert. ■

camera

A **camera** is a thing used to take pictures. It is a small box with a hole to look through.

camp

A **camp** is a place to live outdoors. Mike and his family like to **camp** out. ☼*See the picture.*

Mike and his family like to **camp** out.

can

1. I **can** write my name. **Can** you go to the movie with me?

2. A **can** is something to hold things in. Mom opened up two **cans** of soup for our lunch.

candle

A **candle** is something that makes a light when you burn it. Sue blew out the **candles** on her birthday cake.

candy

Candy is something to eat. It is sweet and tastes good. Jimmy loves to eat chocolate **candy.**

cannot

Joan **cannot** play outside because she has a cold.

can't

Can't means **cannot.** The baby **can't** reach the top of the table. ☼*See the picture.*

cap

A **cap** is something that you wear on your head. Ted had on a red **cap.**

car

A **car** is something that you ride in. It has four wheels and a motor to make it go. Father took us to the beach in a **car.** There were many **cars** on the highway.

card

A **card** is a piece of paper. It has words or pictures on it. Jim sent me a birthday **card.** Some games are played with **cards.**

The baby **can't** reach the top of the table.

Joe takes good **care**
of his pet cat.

care

Care means to worry about something. Jan doesn't **care** if Tim rides her bicycle. Joe takes good **care** of his pet cat. ☼*See the picture.*

careful

Careful means that you think about what you do. If you are **careful** when you cross the street, you look both ways to make sure no cars are coming. Bob did his homework very **carefully. Careless** means that you don't think about what you do. Susan was **careless** when she ran down the stairs, and she fell.

carrot

A **carrot** is something to eat. **Carrots** are long and orange. A **carrot** is a vegetable. ■

carry

Carry means to move something. The mother kangaroo **carries** her baby in a pouch on her stomach. ☼*See the picture.* John **carried** the bag of groceries for his mother.

The mother kangaroo **carries** her baby
in a pouch on her stomach.

cartoon

A **cartoon** is a picture that makes you laugh. Bob and Sally watch **cartoons** on television on Saturday mornings.

cat

A **cat** is an animal. **Cats** have soft fur and a long tail.

catch

Catch means to get hold of something that is moving. The two players tried to **catch** the ball. ☼*See the picture.* That cat **catches** lots of mice. Johnny is the **catcher** on the school baseball team.

catsup

Catsup is something to put on food. It is made of tomatoes. I like to put lots of **catsup** on hamburgers.

caught

Mary **caught** the ball and threw it back to Tim.

cave

A **cave** is a hole in the side of a mountain. The family of bears lived in a **cave.** Long ago people lived in **caves.**

ceiling

A **ceiling** is a part of a room. It is over your head. The light hung from the **ceiling.**

cent

A **cent** is a piece of money. It is made of metal. A **cent** is the same thing as a **penny.** The candy bar cost fifteen **cents.** One hundred **cents** is one dollar.

The two players tried to **catch** the ball.

Mom put the plate of cookies in the **center** of the table.

center

A **center** is a place that is in the middle of something. Mom put the plate of cookies in the **center** of the table. ☼*See the picture.*

cereal

Cereal is something to eat. You put milk and sugar on **cereal.** We eat **cereal** for breakfast.

certain

Certain means that you are very sure of something. Are you **certain** that you closed the door? Bob said that we **certainly** could use his bicycle.

chain

A **chain** is a row of rings that are joined together. Margaret wore a very pretty gold **chain** around her neck. Ted **chained** his dog to the fence so that it couldn't run away. ☼*See the picture.*

Ted **chained** his dog to the fence so that it couldn't run away.

chair

A **chair** is something to sit on. **Chairs** have four legs and a back. Frank sat in the blue **chair** by the fire.

chalk

Chalk is something that is used to write with. It is used to write and draw on a blackboard. The teacher wrote the answer on the blackboard with a piece of yellow **chalk.**

chance

A **chance** is a time to do something. Each child will have a **chance** to ride the pony. ☼*See the picture.*

Each child will have a **chance** to ride the pony.

Mom **changed** the tire because the old one was flat.

change

Change means to make something different from what it is. I have to **change** my clothes before I go out to play. Mom **changed** the tire because the old one was flat. ☼*See the picture.*

channel

A **channel** is a place that sends out television programs. Frank changed the **channel** on the TV set so he could watch the baseball game.

chase

Chase means to run after something. When you **chase** something, you try to catch it. The dog is **chasing** the birds. ☼*See the picture.* Frank **chased** the ball after Joan kicked it.

cheap

When something is **cheap** it means that it does not cost a lot of money. This piece of candy was **cheap;** it only cost two cents.

The dog is **chasing** the birds.

check

Check means to make sure that something is right. Billy **checked** his answers before handing in his homework.

cheek

Your **cheek** is a part of your face. Your **cheeks** are under your eyes. Martha had red paint on her **cheek** after she finished painting the picture.

cheese

Cheese is something to eat. It is made of milk. Betty and Tom ate some **cheese** and crackers for lunch.

cherry

A **cherry** is something to eat. It is small and round. A **cherry** is a red fruit. **Cherries** grow on trees.

chest

1. Your **chest** is a part of your body. Your **chest** is the front of you between your shoulders and your waist. Your heart is in your **chest.**
2. A **chest** is also a big box that holds things. Sam put his truck in the toy **chest** when he finished playing with it. My father keeps his hammer in a tool **chest.**

chew

Chew means to cut something with the teeth. We should **chew** our food slowly. My dog likes to **chew** on an old bone. ☼*See the picture.*

chicken

A **chicken** is a bird. **Chickens** lay eggs that we eat. A **chicken** is good to eat.

My dog likes to **chew** on an old bone.

The skater made a **circle** on the ice.

child

A **child** is a young boy or girl. Billy liked to play in the playground with the other **children** in his class.

chimney

A **chimney** is a part of a house. A **chimney** carries away smoke from a fireplace.

chin

The **chin** is a part of your face. Your **chin** is under your mouth and above your neck.

chocolate

Chocolate is something to eat. It is sweet and tastes good. We gave Mom a box of **chocolate** candy for her birthday.

choose

Choose means to pick out something that you want to have. Billy had to **choose** which balloon he wanted.

Christmas

Christmas is a time of the year. It comes on December 25.

church

A **church** is a building. Some people go to **church** to show their love for God.

circle

A **circle** is something round. The skater made a **circle** on the ice. ☼*See the picture.*

circus

A **circus** is a show. You see people and animals do special things in a **circus.** We went to the **circus** and saw a girl riding an elephant.

city

A **city** is a very large place. Many people live and work there. **Cities** have a lot of big office buildings and apartment houses.

class

A **class** is a group of children that learn the same things together in a school. A **classroom** is a place where a **class** works with the teacher.

claw

A **claw** is a sharp nail. Birds and animals have **claws.** My cat scratched me with her **claws.**

clean

Clean means that something is not dirty. Are your hands **clean?** My brother **cleaned** up his room. The family worked together to **clean** out the garage. ☼*See the picture.*

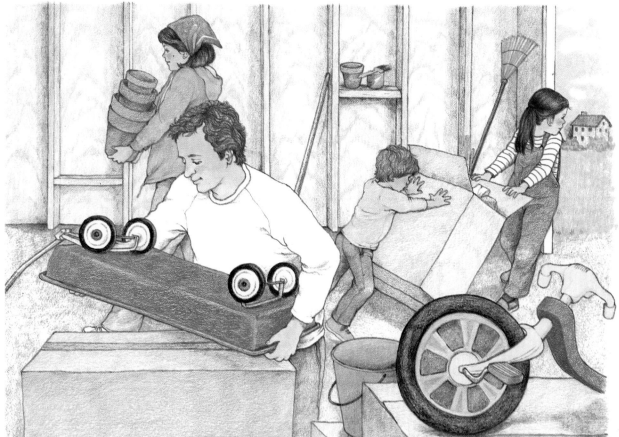

The family worked together to **clean** out the garage.

The squirrel **climbed** quickly up the tree.

clear

Clear means that something is easy to see through. Glass is **clear.** The water in the pond was so **clear** that we could see the fish in it.

climb

Climb means to go up something. The squirrel **climbed** quickly up the tree. ☼*See the picture.*

clock

A **clock** is a thing that shows you what time it is. The **clock** on the wall showed that it was twelve o'clock. ■

close

1. Close means to shut something. I **closed** the window, because my room was too cold.
2. Close also means that something is near something else. The horses were **close** at the end of the race. ☼*See the picture.* My house is **closer** to the school than Jack's is. The mother watched her baby **closely** while he was playing in the yard.

The horses were **close** at the end of the race.

closet

A **closet** is a small room. Clothes and other things are kept in a **closet.**

cloth

Cloth is something that is made from cotton or wool. It is used to make clothes and other things.

clothes

Clothes are the things that we wear. Betty has a coat, dresses, and other **clothes.**

cloud

A **cloud** is a thing that floats high in the sky. It is made of tiny drops of water. There were dark **clouds** in the sky before the rainstorm.

clown

A **clown** is someone who makes you laugh. The **clowns** at the circus wore funny clothes.

coat

A **coat** is something to wear. It is worn over your other clothes when you go outdoors. My winter **coat** keeps me warm. We hung our **coats** in the closet.

coffee

Coffee is something to drink. It is brown. My mother puts sugar in her **coffee.**

cold

1. When something is **cold** it means that it is not warm. Ice is very **cold.** The puppy wanted to come in because she was cold. ☼*See the picture.*
2. A **cold** is also something that makes you feel sick. Tim has a **cold** and has to stay in.

The puppy wanted to come in because she was **cold.**

collar

A **collar** is a thing that you wear around your neck. My dog has a red **collar.**

color

When you **color** a picture, it means that you put red, blue, yellow, green and other **colors** on it. Mary has crayons of many **colors.**

comb

A **comb** is a thing that you use to make your hair smooth. Bob **combed** his hair before he went out.

come

Come means to move toward something. My dog **comes** to me when I call its name. My mother is **coming** to our school fair.

comfortable

Comfortable means that something feels nice. The dog was **comfortable** in his basket. ☼*See the picture.*

The dog was **comfortable** in his basket.

commercial

A **commercial** is something on radio or television. It tells about something that you can buy. The **commercial** showed a woman driving a new car.

We had **company** for dinner on Thanksgiving.

company

Company is someone who visits you. We had **company** for dinner on Thanksgiving. ☼*See the picture.*

contest

A **contest** is a game. You try to win a **contest.** We had a **contest** to see who could throw the ball the highest. Judy won the spelling **contest** at school.

cook

Cook means to do something to food to make it ready to eat. Food gets hot when it is **cooked.** Dad likes **cooking** our dinner on his day off. ☼*See the picture.*

cookie

A **cookie** is something sweet to eat. It is small and flat. Jerry brought a box of chocolate **cookies** to the picnic.

Dad likes **cooking** our dinner on his day off.

Andy tried to make a **copy** of the painting on the wall.

copy

Copy means to do something that is just like something else. Andy tried to make a **copy** of the painting on the wall. ☼*See the picture.*

corn

Corn is something to eat. It is long and yellow and has a green covering. **Corn** is a vegetable.

corner

A **corner** is a place where two things come together. The place where two streets come together is called a **corner.** There was a mouse sitting in the **corner** of the room. ☼*See the picture.*

cost

Cost is a word that is used to tell how much money you can buy something for. How much did your new shoes **cost?**

There was a mouse sitting in the **corner** of the room.

The children all wore **costumes** to the Halloween party.

costume

A **costume** is something to wear. When you wear a **costume** you look like someone else. The children all wore **costumes** to the Halloween party. ☼*See the picture.*

cotton

Cotton is a kind of cloth. It is made from the parts of a plant.

couch

A **couch** is something to sit on. More than one person can sit on a **couch.**

cough

Cough means to make a noise by making air come out of your lungs. Beth stayed home because she has a cold and **coughs** all the time.

The baby deer **couldn't** walk well yet.

could

I **could** tell by Jim's smile that he was happy. **Couldn't** means "could not." The baby deer **couldn't** walk well yet. ☼*See the picture.*

count

Count means to find out how many of something there are. I **counted** how many cookies there were in the box.

country

1. A **country** is a large piece of land and all the people who live there. The United States is a **country**.
2. **Country** also means land that is outside of cities. There are farms and woods in the **country**.

cousin

Your **cousin** is the child of your aunt or uncle. If your aunt and uncle have three children, then you have three **cousins**.

cover

Cover means to put a thing over something else. He **covered** the horse with a blanket to keep it warm. ☼*See the picture.* There is a picture of a house on the **cover** of that book.

cow

A **cow** is an animal. We get milk from **cows.**

cowboy

A **cowboy** is a man who takes care of cows. **Cowboys** ride horses to do their work. The **cowboy** rode all over looking for the lost cow.

crack

A **crack** is a small opening in something. A **crack** does not make a thing fall into pieces. The window has **cracks** in it where my baseball hit it. The plate **cracked** when I hit it against the sink.

cracker

A **cracker** is something to eat. It is like a cookie but it is not sweet. We had some **crackers** with our soup.

crash

Crash means to hit and make a very loud noise. The dog knocked over the table and the lamp on it **crashed** to the floor. There was a **crash** when the ball broke the window.

crawl

Crawl means to go along very slowly on your hands and knees. The baby **crawled** across the floor. ☼*See the picture.*

He **covered** the horse with a blanket to keep it warm.

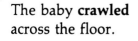

The baby **crawled** across the floor.

53

crayon

A **crayon** is a colored stick. It is used for writing and drawing. **Crayons** come in many colors.

cream

Cream is the thick part of milk. Butter is made from **cream.** I like to put **cream** on my cereal.

crocodile

A **crocodile** is an animal. It has a long body and short legs. It also has a long tail. **Crocodiles** live in the water.

cross

Cross means to move from one side of something to the other. The children **crossed** the street when the policeman told them to. ☼*See the picture.*

The children **crossed** the street when the policeman told them to.

cry

Cry means to have tears come out of your eyes. The baby **cried** because he was hungry. Tommy never **cries** when he falls down.

cup

A **cup** is something to drink from. It has a handle. Susan drank her milk from a **cup.**

cupcake

A **cupcake** is a small cake. **Cupcakes** are good to eat. Mom baked **cupcakes** for our class party.

cut

Cut means to make something into pieces. Laura **cut** the pie into six pieces. Chris got his hair **cut** before he started school this year. ☼*See the picture.* Bill got a small **cut** on his hand from the broken glass.

cute

Cute means that a thing is very nice to look at. The kitten was so **cute** that it made us smile. ☼*See the picture.*

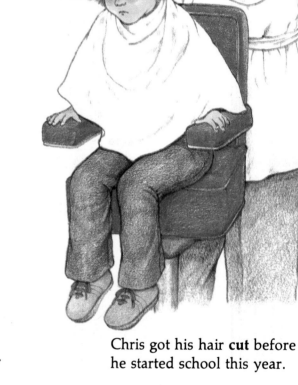

Chris got his hair **cut** before he started school this year.

The kitten was so **cute** that it made us smile.

dictionary   See page 59

drum   See page 66

doll   See page 63

On this page are pictures of words that begin with the letter "D". Can you find each word in your book? Turn to the page number you see near the picture. When you find the right word you will see this: ■

dad

Dad is a name for your father. Some children also call their father **Daddy.**

dance

Dance means to move your body in a special way. You **dance** along with music.

danger

Danger is something that might hurt you. Tom knows the **danger** of crossing the street when the light is red. It is **dangerous** to skate on the pond unless the ice is very thick.
☼*See the picture.*

dark

Dark means that something is not light. It is **dark** outside at night. Nancy has **dark** hair.

daughter

A **daughter** is a child who is a girl or woman. Catherine is the **daughter** of her mother and father.

It is **dangerous** to skate on the pond unless the ice is very thick.

day

1. **Day** is the time when it is light outside. We spent the **day** at the beach.
2. A **day** is also a part of a week. There are seven **days** in a week. A **day** has twenty-four hours.

dead

When something is **dead** it means that it is no longer alive. The plant was **dead** because it did not get enough water.

David couldn't **decide**
which fish to buy
at the pet store.

decide

When you **decide** you make up your mind about something. David couldn't **decide** which fish to buy at the pet store. ☼*See the picture.* Jim **decided** to wear his blue jacket.

deep

When a thing is **deep** it means that it goes far down into something. The children dug a **deep** hole in the sand.

deer

A **deer** is an animal. Some **deer** have horns. **Deer** can run very fast.

delicious

If something is **delicious,** it means that it is very good to eat or smell. The bakery sells lots of **delicious** cookies. ☼*See the picture.*

The bakery sells lots of **delicious** cookies.

dentist

A **dentist** is a kind of doctor. A **dentist** takes care of your teeth.

desert

A **desert** is a place that is covered with sand. It can be very hot in a **desert.**

desk

A **desk** is a kind of table. You read or write at a **desk.** Our classroom has **desks.**

dessert

Dessert is something sweet to eat. Ice cream and cakes are **desserts.** You eat **dessert** after you have eaten the rest of your dinner.

detective

A **detective** is someone who tries to find out things. The **detective's** job was to find out who stole the money.

diamond

A **diamond** is a kind of stone. **Diamonds** are worth a lot of money.

dictionary

A **dictionary** is a kind of book. It tells you what words mean and how they are spelled. ■

did

Did you go to school today? **Didn't** means "did not." The dog **didn't** want to go outside because it was raining. ☼*See the picture.*

The dog **didn't** want to go outside because it was raining.

die

Die means to stop living. The flowers will **die** if you don't water them.

The mother and father ducks look very **different**.

different

When something is **different,** it is not the same as something else. A chair and a table are **different.** The mother and father ducks look very **different.** ☼*See the picture.*

dig

Dig means to make a hole in something. John likes to **dig** in the sand with a shovel.

dime

A **dime** is a piece of money. It is made of metal. A **dime** is the same as ten cents.

dining room

A **dining room** is a place to eat in. It is a room in a house.

dinner

Dinner is food. We eat the biggest meal of the day at **dinner.**

dinosaur

A **dinosaur** was an animal that lived a long, long time ago. It was a very large animal.

dirt

Dirt is something that makes things not clean. Mud and dust are **dirt.** Mike got his clothes **dirty** playing football. ☼*See the picture.*

Mike got his clothes **dirty** playing football.

disappear

When something **disappears** it goes where you cannot see it. The magician made the rabbit in his hat **disappear.** The sun **disappeared** behind a cloud.

disappoint

To **disappoint** means to make someone sad. When something **disappoints** you, you are unhappy because it did not happen. Caroline was **disappointed** that she couldn't go out to play. ☼*See the picture.*

Caroline was **disappointed** that she couldn't go out to play.

discover

Discover means to find something. When you **discover** something you find it for the first time. Joan **discovered** a bird's nest in a tree. ☼*See the picture.*

disguise

Disguise means to hide something. The children wore funny faces to **disguise** themselves on Halloween.

dish

A **dish** is something to put food on. Tom put the food on **dishes.**

dishonest

When you are **dishonest,** it means that you are not telling the truth. If you tell a lie you are **dishonest.**

dive

Dive means to go into the water with your head first. Jean **dove** into the swimming pool.

Joan **discovered** a bird's nest in a tree.

The teacher **divided** the children into two teams for the game.

divide

1. Divide means to make something into parts. Pam **divided** the cake into eight pieces with a knife. The teacher **divided** the children into two teams for the game. ☼*See the picture.*
2. Divide also means to make a number smaller. If you **divide** 6 by 3, you get 2.

do

Karen helped her little brother **do** his homework. ☼*See the picture.* **Don't** means "do not." I **don't** know that boy's name.

doctor

A **doctor** is someone who takes care of sick people and makes them well. Mark's mother took him to the **doctor** when he was sick.

Karen helped her little brother **do** his homework.

does

Does she like to swim? **Doesn't** means "does not." Ellen has an umbrella but Timmy **doesn't.** ☀*See the picture.*

Ellen has an umbrella but Timmy **doesn't.**

dog

A **dog** is an animal. It has fur and it barks. People have **dogs** as pets.

doll

A **doll** is a toy. A **doll** looks like a baby, a child, or a grown-up. ■

dollar

A **dollar** is a piece of money. It is made of paper. A **dollar** is the same as one hundred cents. That book costs six **dollars.**

My homework is all **done.**

done

My homework is all **done.** ☼*See the picture.*

door

A **door** is a thing that opens or shuts the way into a place. Rooms and closets have **doors.**

dot

A **dot** is a small spot. Mary has a new dress that is white with blue **dots.**

double

Double means that there are two of a thing.

down

When you go **down,** you go from a high place to a lower place. Chuck fell **down** and hurt his knee. The chipmunk jumped **down** from the tree. ☼*See the picture.*

dragon

A **dragon** is a big animal. It has wings and sends out fire from its mouth. **Dragons** are not real.

drank

Larry **drank** two glasses of water because he was thirsty.

draw

Draw means to make a picture of something. The teacher told us to **draw** a picture of a clown with our crayons. Mom put Howard's **drawing** up on the wall.

drawer

A **drawer** is a box that you can push in and pull out. If you open the kitchen **drawer** you will find the spoons.

The chipmunk jumped **down** from the tree.

dream

Dream means to have pictures in your mind when you are asleep. Carol **dreamed** last night that she could fly. Al had a **dream** about riding a horse.

dress

A **dress** is something to wear. Girls and women wear **dresses.** A **dress** has a top and a skirt that are sewed together. My little sister is learning to get **dressed** by herself.

drink

Drink means to put something into your mouth and swallow it. Milk and water are things to **drink.** The elephants are **drinking** from the river. ☼*See the picture.*

The elephants are **drinking** from the river.

Phil **dropped** his glass of
milk on the kitchen floor.

drive

Drive means to use a car. Mom **drives** to
work every morning. The bus **drove** us home
from school.

drop

Drop means to let something fall. Phil
dropped his glass of milk on the kitchen floor.
☼*See the picture.* Rain is **drops** of water that
fall from the sky.

drum

A **drum** is something that makes a sound
when you hit it. My sister plays the **drums** in
the school band. ■

dry

Dry means that something has no water in it.
We hung our clothes on the line to **dry**. ☼*See
the picture.* Frank washed the dishes and Karen
dried them.

We hung our clothes on the line to **dry**.

The children **dug** a hole in the sand.

dug
The children **dug** a hole in the sand. ☼*See the picture.*

dump
Dump means to drop something. The truck is going to **dump** the dirt by the road.

during
My brother goes to camp **during** the summer. The telephone rang **during** the night.

dust
Dust is very small pieces of dirt. There is **dust** on the table. Mother will **dust** the table with a cloth.

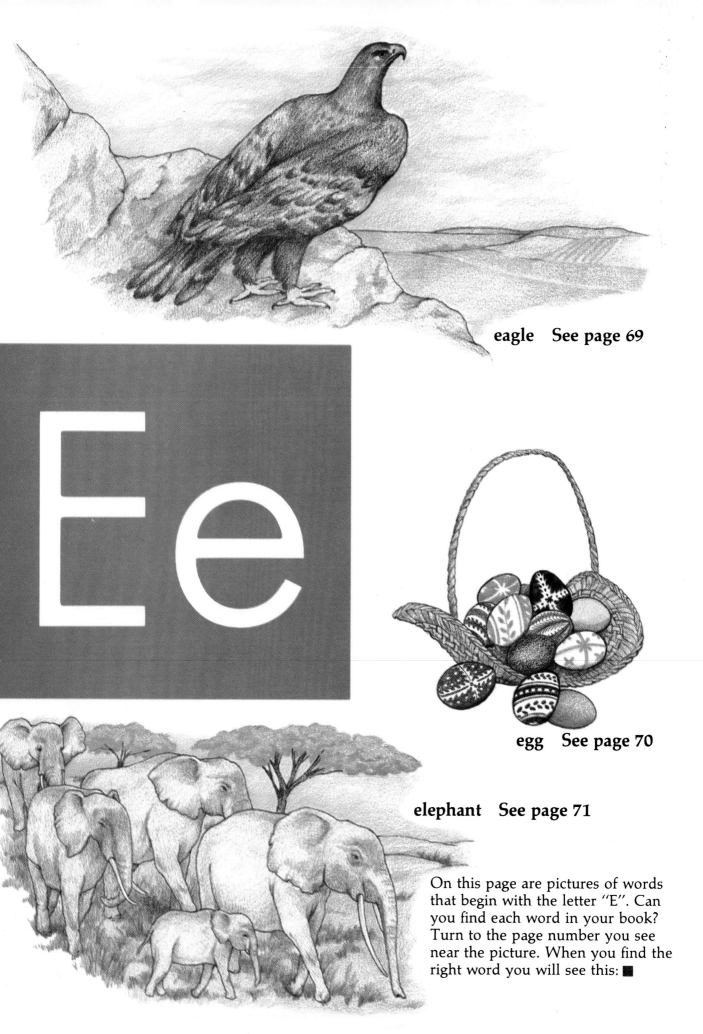

eagle   See page 69

egg   See page 70

elephant   See page 71

On this page are pictures of words that begin with the letter "E". Can you find each word in your book? Turn to the page number you see near the picture. When you find the right word you will see this: ■

each

I gave a piece of cake to **each** of my friends. These candies are ten cents **each. Each** monkey was eating a banana. ☼*See the picture.*

eagle

An **eagle** is a large bird. **Eagles** have very strong claws and large wings. ■

ear

1. The **ear** is a part of your body. You have an **ear** on each side of your head. You hear things with your **ears.**
2. An **ear** is also a part of a plant. Corn grows on **ears.**

early

Early means near the beginning of something. The rooster gets up **early** in the morning. ☼*See the picture.*

earn

Earn means to get money for doing something. My brother **earns** fifty cents for cutting our lawn.

earth

1. The **earth** is where all people live. The **earth** is a planet.
2. **Earth** also means dirt. The farmer planted the seeds in the **earth.**

east

The **east** is the place where the sun comes up in the morning.

Easter

Easter is a time of year. It comes on a Sunday in March or April.

Each monkey was eating a banana.

The rooster gets up **early** in the morning.

It was **easy** for Billy to tell which mittens
were his because they had his name on them.

Mike stood on the **edge**
of the diving board.

easy

When something is **easy,** it is not hard to do.
It was **easy** for Billy to tell which mittens were
his because they had his name on them. ☼*See
the picture.*

eat

Eat means to put food in your mouth and
chew and swallow it. Our dog **eats** his food
very fast. Have you **eaten** lunch yet?

edge

An **edge** is the end part of something. Ted's
pencil rolled off the **edge** of his desk. Mike
stood on the **edge** of the diving board. ☼*See
the picture.*

egg

An **egg** is something that holds a baby bird
until it is ready to be born. All birds lay **eggs.**
A chicken's **egg** is good to eat. ■

either

You may have **either** ice cream or cake. Billy didn't like **either** jacket. ☼*See the picture.*

elbow

The **elbow** is a part of your body. Your **elbow** is where your arm bends.

election

In an **election** we decide whether we are for or against something. We vote in an **election**. There is an **election** for President every four years in the United States.

electricity

Electricity is something that can make motors go. It can also give light and heat. **Electricity** makes television sets and telephones work. **Electric** means that something is made to go by **electricity**. We have an **electric** stove in our kitchen.

Billy didn't like **either** jacket.

elementary school

Elementary school is a school that comes after kindergarten.

elephant

An **elephant** is a very large animal. It is gray and has a long nose, called a trunk. ▪

elevator

An **elevator** is a thing that can carry you up and down in a building. Jerry took the **elevator** up to the sixth floor of the store.

else

Who **else** wants to play baseball? What **else** do you want for lunch? Marcia's mother said, "Hurry up or **else** you'll be late."

empty

If a thing is **empty** it means that there is nothing in it. Jane still has some milk, but Sarah's glass is **empty.** ☼*See the picture.*

Jane still has some milk, but Sarah's glass is **empty.**

end

The **end** is the last part of something. Barbara held on to one **end** of the jump rope and I held on to the other **end.** The book had a happy **ending.** That television program **ends** at nine o'clock. The teacher **ended** the reading lesson just before recess.

engine

An **engine** is something that makes a thing go. The **engine** of a car makes the car move.

engineer

An **engineer** is someone who drives a train. The **engineer** blew the whistle as the train came into the station.

There was **enough** ice cream so that each child could have some.

enough

If you have **enough** of something, you have as much as you need. There was **enough** ice cream so that each child could have some. ☼*See the picture.*

enter

Enter means to go into a place. You **enter** a room through a door.

eraser

An **eraser** is something you use to rub out marks. Lucy cleaned the blackboard with an **eraser.**

escalator

An **escalator** is a set of steps that moves up or down. Tom and his mother took an **escalator** up to the third floor of the store.

escape

Escape means to get away from something. The bird **escaped** from its cage. ☼*See the picture.*

The bird **escaped** from its cage.

73

even

1. When something is **even** it means that it is flat. The floor of a room is **even.**
2. Sally can run **even** faster than Billy.

evening

Evening is a time of day. It starts getting dark in the **evening. Evening** is between afternoon and night.

ever

Have you **ever** been on an airplane? How did Joan **ever** climb that tall tree?

Every goat was eating grass.

every

Every goat was eating grass. ☼*See the picture.* **Everybody** in the family went on the picnic. **Everyone** had a good time at the party. I ate **everything** on my plate. Betty looked **everywhere** in the house for her shoes.

evil

If something is **evil** it means that it is very, very bad. The **evil** witch in the story turned the prince into a frog.

excellent

If something is **excellent,** it means that it is very, very good. Carol is doing **excellent** work in reading at school.

except

All the children like corn **except** Joe. ☼*See the picture.* Jim would go to the playground with us, **except** that he has a cold.

All the children like corn **except** Joe.

excited

When you are **excited** you are very happy about something. June was **excited** when she saw her new puppy. ☼*See the picture.*

excuse

Excuse means to let someone do something. The teacher **excused** Jill from the room. Jimmy brought Mrs. Clark an **excuse** from his mother telling why he was late for school.

exercise

When you **exercise** you move your body in a special way. **Exercise** can make you feel better. Running is a good **exercise.**

exit

An **exit** is a way out of a place. The door of a bus is an **exit.**

expect

Expect means to look forward to something. Barbara **expects** to finish her work soon.

June was **excited** when she saw her new puppy.

Dad didn't want to buy the car because it was very **expensive**.

expensive

When something is **expensive** it means that it costs a lot of money. Dad didn't want to buy the car because it was very **expensive.** ☼*See the picture.*

explain

Explain means to tell someone about something. When you **explain** a thing you make another person understand it. June had to **explain** to Jim how to work the train set.

explore

Explore means to look around a place. Nancy and Robert wanted to **explore** the old, empty house, but their mother wouldn't let them. Christopher Columbus was an **explorer** of America.

extra

If something is **extra,** it is more than you need. Each child got a candy bar, and there was one **extra.** ☼*See the picture.* Mom made an **extra** large cake for my birthday party.

Each child got a candy bar, and there was one **extra.**

eye

The **eye** is a part of your body. You see with your **eyes.** We all have two **eyes.** Your **eyesight** is how you see. The doctor tested Judy's **eyesight** and said that it was good. The line of hair that grows above each of your **eyes** is called an **eyebrow.**

frog   See page 93

Ff

flag   See page 88

On this page are pictures of words that begin with the letter "F". Can you find each word in your book? Turn to the page number you see near the picture. When you find the right word you will see this: ■

fairy   See page 80

face

The **face** is the front part of your head. Your eyes, nose, and mouth are on your **face.** Sue had a smile on her **face.**

fact

A **fact** is something that is true. It is a **fact** that we all live on the earth.

factory

A **factory** is a place where things are made. Cars are made in **factories.**

fair

1. When something is **fair** it means that it is the right thing to do. Janice was **fair** when she gave everyone a cookie.
2. A **fair** is also a place that is fun to go to. People bring things to sell to **fairs.** We bought some cookies at the school **fair.** ☼*See the picture.*

We bought some cookies at the school **fair.**

Snow was **falling** on the ground.

fairy

A **fairy** is someone who can do magic things. **Fairies** are not real. ■

fall

1. **Fall** means to come down from a place that is high. Be careful or you will **fall** out of the tree. Snow was **falling** on the ground. ☼*See the picture.*

2. **Fall** is also a time of the year. It comes between summer and winter.

false

When something is **false,** it means that it is not true. Is it true or **false** that you live in the United States?

family

Your **family** is your mother and your father, and your brothers and sisters. Two new **families** have moved in on our block. A **family** of geese lives in the pond. ☼ *See the picture.*

A **family** of geese lives in the pond.

famous

When someone is **famous** it means that a lot of people know who he or she is. George Washington is a **famous** person.

far

When something is **far** it means that it is not close to you. My grandmother lives **far** away. How **far** is your school from your house?

farm

A **farm** is a piece of land. Things to eat come from **farms**. Joe's family grows corn on their **farm**. Someone who lives on a **farm** is called a **farmer**.

Jan's toy plane went **farther** than Tommy's did.

farther

Jan's toy plane went **farther** than Tommy's did. ☼*See the picture.* Peter lives the **farthest** from school of any boy in my class.

fast

When you are **fast** it means that you can go very quickly. That animal can run very **fast**. ☼*See the picture.* An airplane is **faster** than a car.

That animal can run very **fast**.

fat

When something is **fat** it means that it is big around. Our cat is **fat** because she eats too much.

father

Your **father** is one of your parents. Your **father** is a man.

faucet

A **faucet** is a thing used to turn water on and off. A sink has a **faucet**.

fault

When something you have done is wrong, it means that it is your **fault**. I threw the ball at the window, so it is my **fault** that the window broke.

favor

A **favor** is something nice that you do for someone else. I did Jane a **favor** by lending her my roller skates. All the children got balloons as **favors** at the party.

favorite

Favorite is a word you use to show that you like a thing better than anything else. My little sister always takes her **favorite** doll to bed with her. ☼*See the picture.*

feather

A **feather** is a thing that grows on a bird's skin. **Feathers** help keep a bird warm. That bird has beautiful red **feathers.**

feed

Feed means to give food to someone. Jerry **fed** his baby brother. A mother bird **feeds** her babies. ☼*See the picture.*

My little sister always takes her **favorite** doll to bed with her.

feel

1. Feel means to know that something is touching you. I can **feel** the rain on my face. Jan likes **feeling** her kitten's soft fur.
2. Feel also means to be something. Do you **feel** sick? Jimmy **felt** tired after running so hard. Fred **feels** happy today because he is going to the circus.

feet

Feet means more than one foot. A cat has four **feet.** Joan is almost five **feet** tall.

A mother bird **feeds** her babies.

Nancy **fell** on the ice while she was skating.

fell
Nancy **fell** on the ice while she was skating.
☼*See the picture.*

female
A **female** is a girl or woman. Your mother is a **female**.

fence
A **fence** is something that is put around something else. There is a wooden **fence** around our back yard to keep the dog from getting out.

fever
When you have a **fever** your body feels very hot. If you have a **fever** you are sick.

few

Few is a word used to show that there are not many of something. There were only a **few** cows in the field. ☼*See the picture.*

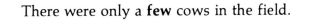

There were only a **few** cows in the field.

field

A **field** is a flat piece of land. Corn is grown in a **field.** Football is played on a **field.**

fierce

When something is **fierce** it means that it is very mean. A hungry lion is **fierce.**

fight

A **fight** is something that happens when you are angry with someone. I had a **fight** with my sister because she lost my ball. Mom told me that I shouldn't have **fought** with her.

fill

Fill means to make something full of a thing. Bob **filled** his pail with sand. ☼*See the picture.*

Bob **filled** his pail with sand.

85

Greg **found** his baseball glove.

find

Find means to come upon something. Jean couldn't **find** her dime on the floor. Greg **found** his baseball glove. ☼ *See the picture.*

fine

When something is **fine** it means that it is good. This is a **fine** day for playing a game of baseball.

finger

A **finger** is a part of your hand. You have five **fingers** at the end of each hand. A **fingernail** is the hard part on the end of each **finger.**

The dog **finished** eating before the cat did.

finish

Finish means to come to the end of something. The dog **finished** eating before the cat did. ☼*See the picture.*

fire

A **fire** is something that is burning. It is hot. A **fire** burned down the old house. A **fireplace** is a place where **fires** can be made indoors.

firecracker

A **firecracker** is something that makes a loud noise. People light **firecrackers** on the Fourth of July.

fire engine

A **fire engine** is a truck. It carries the things needed to put out a fire. Firemen ride on a **fire engine.**

fireman

A **fireman** is someone who puts out fires. A **fireman** is also called a **firefighter.**

first

When something is **first** it means that it comes before everything else. Mary was **first** in line. ☼*See the picture.* "A" is the **first** letter of the alphabet.

Mary was **first** in line.

fish

A **fish** is an animal. It lives in the water. Some **fish** are good to eat. Dad and I are going **fishing** in the lake. Don is a good **fisherman.**

fist

A **fist** is something you make with your hand. To make a **fist** you close your hand tightly into a ball.

Mike's old jacket doesn't **fit** him any more.

fit

Fit means to be the right size. When something **fits** it is not too big or too small. Mike's old jacket doesn't **fit** him any more. ☼*See the picture.*

fix

Fix means to make something like it was. Dad tried to **fix** the wagon. ☼*See the picture.*

Dad tried to **fix** the wagon.

flag

A **flag** is a piece of cloth. It has different colors and pictures on it. Every country has a **flag.** The **flag** of the United States is red, white, and blue. ■

flame

A **flame** is the light you see in a fire. We could see the **flames** from the burning house.

flashlight

A **flashlight** is a thing that gives light. It is small enough to carry in your hand.

flat

Flat means that something is smooth. If something is **flat** it has no bumps. The top of a table is **flat.**

flavor

The **flavor** of something is the way it tastes. Sugar has a sweet **flavor.**

flew

The bird **flew** away when it saw the cat.

float

Float means to move along slowly in the water or in the air. The boat was **floating** in the water. ☼*See the picture.* We let the balloon go and it **floated** over the house.

floor

A **floor** is a part of a room. It is what you walk or stand on. The book fell to the **floor.** Dave's room is on the second **floor.**

flour

Flour is something that is used in making food. It is used to make bread and cake.

flower

A **flower** is a part of a plant. **Flowers** come in many different colors. They are pretty to look at and nice to smell. Roses are **flowers.**

flu

The **flu** is something that makes you feel sick. It is like a very bad cold.

The boat was **floating** in the water.

fly

1. Fly means to move through the air with wings. Birds **fly.** Ben saw an airplane **flying** in the sky.

2. A **fly** is also an insect. **Flies** have two wings.

fold

Fold means to bend one part of a thing over another part. Judy **folded** the piece of paper in half.

The baby bears are **following** their mother.

follow

Follow means to come after something. The baby bears are **following** their mother. ☼*See the picture.* Spring **follows** winter.

food

Food is what we eat. All living things need **food** to help them grow. Bread is an important **food.**

foot

1. Your **foot** is a part of your body. Your **foot** is at the end of your leg. We have two **feet.** We walk and stand on our **feet.**

2. A **foot** is also a word that is used to show how long something is. One **foot** is the same as twelve inches.

football

Football is a game. It is played by two teams. **Football** is played with a ball.

footprint

A **footprint** is a mark made by a foot or shoe. The children made **footprints** on the floor with their dirty boots. ☼*See the picture.*

The children made **footprints** on the floor with their dirty boots.

for

We went **for** a ride in the car. This box is **for** toys. Sarah got a doll **for** her birthday.

forever

Forever means that something will never end. The man in the story wished that he would live **forever.**

forget

Forget means to not remember something. Joe wrote down my address so he would not **forget** it. Dad **forgot** his lunch box when he left for work. ☼*See the picture.*

Dad **forgot** his lunch box when he left for work.

91

forgive

Forgive means to stop being mad at someone. Larry asked his sister to **forgive** him for pushing her.

fork

A **fork** is a thing that you eat food with. It is long with points at one end.

Bill stepped **forward** to get his prize for winning the spelling contest.

forward

Forward means that something is going ahead. The truck moved **forward**. Everyone is looking **forward** to summer vacation. Bill stepped **forward** to get his prize for winning the spelling contest. ☼*See the picture.*

free

Free means that you do not have to pay any money to get something. The magic show in the park is **free.**

freeze

Freeze means to make something very cold. When water **freezes,** it becomes ice. The pond will **freeze** during the winter and we will be able to skate on the ice.

fresh

When something is **fresh** it means that it is new. June brought us some **fresh** vegetables from her garden.

friend

A **friend** is someone you like very much. It is fun to be with a **friend.** Karen and Nancy are good **friends.**

friendly

When someone is **friendly** it means that they are nice to you. Everyone was **friendly** to the new girl in the class. Betty's dogs are very **friendly.** ☼*See the picture.*

Betty's dogs are very **friendly**.

frighten

Frighten means to make someone afraid. The cat **frightened** the birds.

frog

A **frog** is an animal. It is small and hops from place to place. **Frogs** live in the water. ■

from

We walked home **from** school. I took a cookie **from** the jar. One **from** three leaves two.

All the children wanted to sit in the **front** seat.

front

The **front** is the part that faces forward. There is a big tree in **front** of my house. All the children wanted to sit in the **front** seat. ☼*See the picture.*

frown

Frown means to push your eyebrows down. You **frown** when you are angry or when you are thinking hard. Bud had a **frown** on his face when his sister yelled at him. Sharon **frowned** when she couldn't think of the answer to the puzzle.

fruit

A **fruit** is something to eat. It is a part of a plant. An apple is a **fruit** that grows on a tree. A strawberry is a **fruit** that grows on a bush. Bananas, oranges, and lemons are also **fruits.**

full

Full means that something is holding as much as it can. When something is **full,** nothing else can be put in it. The jar was **full** of candy. ☼*See the picture.*

The jar was **full** of candy.

fun

When you are having **fun** it means that you are having a good time. You laugh and play when you have **fun.** The children had **fun** riding their sleds down the hill.

The **funny** clown made the children laugh.

funny

When something is **funny** it makes you laugh. The **funny** clown made the children laugh. ☼*See the picture.*

fur

Fur is the hair that covers an animal's body.

furnace

A **furnace** is a closed place that heat comes out of. **Furnaces** are used to heat houses.

furniture

Tables, chairs, and beds are part of the **furniture** in your house.

goose   See page 101

giraffe   See page 99

Gg

gorilla   See page 101

On this page are pictures of words that begin with the letter "G". Can you find each word in your book? Turn to the page number you see near the picture. When you find the right word you will see this: ■

goat   See page 100

game

A **game** is something you play. The children played a **game** of hide-and-seek.

garage

A **garage** is a place where cars are kept. Ned and Jane keep their bicycles in the **garage.**

garbage

Garbage is food that is left over after a meal. We throw **garbage** away.

garden

A **garden** is a place where flowers or vegetables grow. Ted and Karen grow tomatoes in their **garden.** ☼*See the picture.*

gas

Gas is something that is put into a machine to make it work. One kind of **gas** is put into a car to make it go. This kind of **gas** is also called **gasoline.** Another kind of **gas** is put into stoves for cooking.

gate

A **gate** is a thing that opens or shuts the way into a place. A **gate** is in a fence. Jim forgot to close the **gate** and the dog got out of the yard.

Tod and Karen grow tomatoes in their **garden.**

gather

Gather means to bring together. The children **gathered** their books and left for school.

Pat **gave** the horse an apple.

gave
Pat **gave** the horse an apple. ☼*See the picture.*

gentle
When someone is **gentle,** it means that they are very careful not to hurt. Joan is **gentle** when she plays with her baby brother.

get
Mary hopes to **get** a watch for her birthday. My older brother **gets** home from school later than I do. Our puppy is **getting** bigger.

ghost
A **ghost** is a thing that some people believe comes back after someone has died. **Ghosts** are not real. The children dressed up as **ghosts** for Halloween.

giant
A **giant** is something that is very, very big. A whale is a **giant** animal. ☼*See the picture.*

A whale is a **giant** animal.

giraffe

A **giraffe** is a very tall animal. It has a very long neck and spots on its skin. ■

girl

A **girl** is a child who will grow up to be a woman. **Girls** are female children.

give

Give means to let someone have something to keep. Ellen's parents are going to **give** her a bicycle for her birthday. Mom **gives** my clothes to my little sister when I grow out of them.

glad

When you feel **glad** it means you are happy. Mrs. Peters was **glad** to see her friends. ☼*See the picture.*

Mrs. Peters was **glad** to see her friends.

glass

Glass is something that you can see through. It is hard and you can break it. Windows are made of **glass**. A **glass** is also something you drink out of. The things that some people wear in front of their eyes to see better are called **glasses**.

glove

A **glove** is something you wear on your hand. **Gloves** have parts that cover your fingers.

glue

Glue is something that makes things stick together. Mike **glued** the wings on the airplane he was making. ☼*See the picture.*

Mike **glued** the wings on the airplane he was making.

Jenny will **go** first in the game.

go

Go means to move from one place to another. Ned and Janet have to **go** home now. Ellen has to **go** to sleep early on school nights. This street **goes** to the beach. I think it is **going** to rain this afternoon. Jenny will **go** first in the game. ☼*See the picture.*

goat

A **goat** is an animal. It has horns and a little piece of hair under its chin that looks like a beard. ◼

God

Many people believe that **God** is the one that made the world and everything in it. Christians, Jews, and Muslims have this idea of **God.** People show their love for **God** in many ways.

good

When something is **good,** it means that it is not bad. The cake is **good.** Jack watched a **good** television program. The children were **good** all day at school. Chuck is a **good** fisherman. ☼*See the picture.*

good-by

Good-by is something you say when you are going away. The children said **good-by** to their mother when they left for school.

goose

A **goose** is a bird. **Geese** can swim. ■

gorilla

A **gorilla** is a large animal. It is a kind of monkey. **Gorillas** have short legs and long arms. ■

got

Billy **got** a new drum for his birthday. ☼*See the picture.*

government

The **government** is what rules a country. The President is the leader of the **government** in the United States.

grade

A **grade** is a year of work in school. My sister is in the first **grade.**

grandparent

Your **grandparents** are your mother and father's parents. Your **grandfather** is your father or mother's father. Your **grandmother** is your mother or father's mother. You are their **granddaughter** or **grandson.**

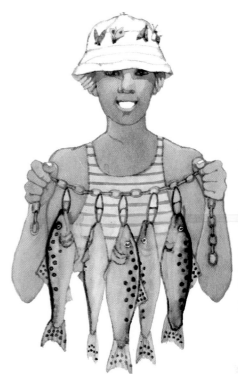

Chuck is a **good** fisherman.

Billy **got** a new drum for his birthday.

grass

Grass is a green plant. **Grass** grows in lawns and fields. Horses, cows, sheep, and other animals eat **grass.**

grasshopper

A **grasshopper** is an insect. A **grasshopper** has long back legs that it uses for jumping.

A **great** number of birds came to the pond.

great

Great means large. A **great** number is a large number. A **great** number of birds came to the pond. ☼ *See the picture.*

grocery

A **grocery** is a place that sells food. The man put the **groceries** into a large paper bag.

ground

Ground is the hard part of the earth. Snow covered the **ground.**

group

A **group** is a number of people that are together. A **group** of children played ball.

grow

Grow means to get larger. The plant **grew** quickly after I watered it. Sam wants to be a doctor when he **grows** up. Lisa has **grown** two inches in the last year. ☼*See the picture.* We are **growing** tomatoes in the back yard.

growl

Growl means to make a sound like a dog. Dogs **growl** when they are angry.

grown-up

A **grown-up** is someone who has finished growing. Your parents are **grown-ups.**

guess

Guess means to try to think of the answer to something. When you **guess,** you are not very sure that your answer is right. Ellen tried to **guess** who was behind her. ☼*See the picture.*

guest

A **guest** is someone who comes to visit you.

gun

A **gun** is a thing that shoots bullets.

gym

A **gym** is a place in a school. It is a place where you play games and do exercises.

Lisa has **grown** two inches in the last year.

Ellen tried to **guess** who was behind her.

103

horse   See page 115

hamburger   See page 105

On this page are pictures of words that begin with the letter "H". Can you find each word in your book? Turn to the page number you see near the picture. When you find the right word you will see this: ■

hippopotamus   See page 113

habit

A **habit** is something that you do without thinking about it. My little sister has the **habit** putting her thumb in her mouth all the time.

had

We **had** fun at the party. The dog **had** to wear a sweater when he went out. ☼*See the picture.* **Hadn't** means "had not." I **hadn't** ever seen that movie before.

The dog **had** to wear a sweater when he went out.

hair

Hair is what grows on your skin. You have **hair** on your head. Laura's **hair** is brown. Our dog has long black **hair.**

half

A **half** is one part of something. When you cut something in **half** it means that you cut it into two parts that are the same size. Bruce ate **half** a grapefruit for breakfast. ☼*See the picture.*

hall

A **hall** is a way for getting from one room to another in a building. The students lined up in the **hall** before they went into the cafeteria for lunch.

Halloween

We get dressed up in funny clothes and play tricks on **Halloween. Halloween** comes on October 31.

hamburger

A **hamburger** is something to eat. It is made from meat that is cut up. I like to eat my **hamburger** on a roll with lots of catsup. ■

Bruce ate **half** a grapefruit for breakfast.

Jack **hammered** the nails into the piece of wood.

hammer

A **hammer** is a thing to hit a nail with. It has a long handle with a piece of metal on one end. Jack **hammered** the nails into the piece of wood. ☼*See the picture.*

hamster

A **hamster** is an animal. It looks something like a mouse. **Hamsters** have fat bodies.

hand

Your **hand** is a part of your body. Your **hand** is at the end of your arm. We have two **hands.** We use our **hands** to pick up and hold things. Please **hand** me the book.

handle

A **handle** is a part that you use to hold on to something with. It is held by your hand. A cup has a **handle.**

handsome

When a boy or man is **handsome,** it means that he is nice to look at. My father is **handsome.**

hang

Hang means to hold something from above. Did you **hang** your clothes up? The monkey is **hanging** by its tail. ☼*See the picture.*

hanger

A **hanger** is something to hang clothes on. **Hangers** can be made of wire or wood. I hung my coat on a **hanger** in the closet.

happen

Happen means to take place. What **happened** in school today?

happy

When you are **happy** it means that you feel very good about something. I was **happy** to see my grandmother. The players were **happy** because they won the game. ☼*See the picture.*

The monkey is **hanging** by its tail.

The players were **happy** because they won the game.

hard

1. When something is **hard** it means that it is not soft. Rocks are **hard.**

2. When something is **hard** it also means that it is not easy to do. This puzzle is **hard** to do.

The bird **has** a beautiful tail.

has

Betty **has** a new bicycle. Jerry **has** a cold. The bird **has** a beautiful tail. ☼*See the picture.* **Hasn't** means "has not." Lou **hasn't** seen my book anywhere.

hat

A **hat** is a thing to wear on your head.

hate

Hate means to not like something very much. Julia **hates** to clean up her room.

have

Jimmy and his friend both **have** new toy trucks. ☼*See the picture.* I **have** to help my brother clean up our room. We are **having** a picnic tomorrow. **Haven't** means "have not." We **haven't** eaten lunch yet.

Jimmy and his friend both **have** new toy trucks.

he

Bob said that **he** wanted something to eat. **He'd** means "he had." **He'd** never been to the circus before. **He'll** means "he will." **He'll** come to my party. **He's** means "he is." **He's** my best friend.

head

Your **head** is the top part of your body. Your eyes, ears, nose, and mouth are parts of your **head.** Your brain is in your **head.** Bobby was at the **head** of the line.

hear

Hear means to get sounds through your ears. I **hear** someone calling my name. Please speak louder, I can't **hear** you. I **heard** thunder before it started to rain.

heart

Your **heart** is a part of your body. It is in your chest. Your **heart** sends blood to all the parts of your body.

heat

Heat means to make something hot. Mom **heated** the milk before giving it to the baby. The fire in the fireplace **heated** the room. The sun gives **heat.** We turned on the electric **heater** because it was so cold in the room.

heaven

Heaven is the place where God lives. It is in the sky.

heavy

When something is **heavy** it means that it is hard to pick up. The bag was too **heavy** for Steve to lift. ☼*See the picture.*

The bag was too **heavy** for Steve to lift.

heel

Your **heel** is a part of your foot. It is on the back of your foot under your ankle. Your **heel** goes into the back part of your shoe.

height

Height is how far something is from the ground. John's **height** is four feet.

held

The mother lion **held** her baby by the back of its neck. ☼*See the picture.*

The mother lion **held** her baby by the back of its neck.

helicopter

A **helicopter** is a thing that flies through the air. It has an engine to make it go. It also has moving parts on top that help it stay in the air.

hello

Hello is something you say when you see someone. I said **hello** to John when I met him in the store.

The children **helped** their father shovel the snow.

help

Help means to do something for someone
else. The children **helped** their father shovel
the snow. ☼*See the picture.* Please tell me if
you need **help** washing the dishes.

hen

A **hen** is a mother chicken. **Hens** lay eggs.

her

Betty's friends came to visit **her. Her** coat is
on the chair. Is this coat **hers?** Ann hurt
herself when she fell down.

here

Here means that something is in this place. Bring the book **here.**

hide

Hide means to put something in a place where it cannot be seen. Bill tried to **hide** behind a tree, but the others found him. Mary **hid** the money she saved in a box under her bed. The dog has **hidden** his bone.

high

When something is **high** it means that it is far from the ground. That animal can jump very **high.** ☼*See the picture.*

That animal can jump very **high.**

hill

A **hill** is a high piece of land. A **hill** is not as high as a mountain.

him

Bill asked me to help **him.** She gave a piece of candy to **him.** Timmy walked home by **himself.**

hippopotamus

A **hippopotamus** is an animal. It is very big. It has short legs and thick skin with no hair on it. **Hippopotamuses** live near water. ■

his

This is my book and that one is **his.** Ted's book has **his** name on it.

hit

Hit means to touch hard against something. Jack **hit** me on the back with his hand. Sandy **hit** the ball hard. ☼*See the picture.*

Sandy **hit** the ball hard.

hold

Hold means to keep something in a place. Mother let me **hold** my baby sister in my arms. The school bus **holds** fifty people.

hole

A **hole** is an open place in something. There are **holes** in these old socks. The dog dug a **hole** in the ground to hide his bone.

The fox hid inside a **hollow** log.

hollow

When something is **hollow** it means that it has an empty place inside. My ball is **hollow.** The fox hid inside a **hollow** log. ☼*See the picture.*

home

Home is the place where you live. Sarah's **home** is the red house next to mine.

homework

Homework is school work that you do at home. The teacher gave us some **homework.**

honest

When someone is **honest** it means that they always tell the truth. Jerry is a very **honest** boy. It is not **honest** to steal something.

honey

Honey is something to eat. It is made by bees. **Honey** is sweet and thick. I like to eat **honey** on bread.

hop

Hop means to make a short jump on your feet. The frog **hopped** into the water. ☼*See the picture.*

hope

Hope means to want something very much. I **hope** that tomorrow is a sunny day so we can go to the beach.

horn

1. A **horn** is something that you blow. Some **horns** make music when you blow into them. Cars have **horns** that make a loud noise. The bus driver blew his **horn** at the children in the street.
2. A **horn** is also a pointed part on the head of an animal. Cows and deer have **horns.**

horse

A **horse** is a big animal. A **horse** has four legs and a long, pretty tail. People can ride **horses.** ■

hospital

A **hospital** is a place where sick people go to get better. Doctors and nurses work in **hospitals.**

hot

When something is **hot,** it means that it burns when you touch or taste it. Earl burned his hand when he touched the **hot** iron. When my dog gets **hot** in the summer, he likes to stand in the water. ☼*See the picture.*

The frog **hopped** into the water.

When my dog gets **hot** in the summer, he likes to stand in the water.

hot dog

A **hot dog** is something to eat. It is long and round and made of meat. John likes to eat his **hot dog** on a roll.

hotel

A **hotel** is a building with a lot of rooms. People sleep in a **hotel** when they are away from home.

hour

An **hour** is a part of a day. There are twenty-four **hours** in a day. An **hour** is the same as sixty minutes.

house

A **house** is a place where people live. Dave asked us to his **house** to play. There are ten **houses** on our street.

how

How cold is it outside? **How** did you like the story? **How** are you today? **How** old is he?

hug

Hug means to put your arms around someone and hold them tightly. You **hug** someone to show them that you love them. The boys **hugged** their grandmother because they were so glad to see her. ☼*See the picture.*

The boys **hugged** their grandmother because they were so glad to see her.

huge

When something is **huge** it means that it is very, very big. An elephant is a **huge** animal.

human

A **human** is a person. Every man, woman and child is a **human.** Men, women, and children are **human** beings.

The children **hung** up their stockings by the fireplace.

hung

The children **hung** up their stockings by the fireplace. ☼*See the picture.*

hungry

When you are **hungry** it means that you want something to eat. Fred was **hungry** all morning because he didn't eat breakfast.

hurry

Hurry means to move fast. Nancy had to **hurry** to catch the school bus. ☼*See the picture.*

hurt

Hurt means to make something feel sore. Kevin fell on the floor and **hurt** his arm. My stomach **hurts.** Larry **hurt** Ben's feelings when he laughed at him.

husband

A **husband** is a man who is married. Your father is your mother's **husband.**

Nancy had to **hurry** to catch the school bus.

ice   See page 119

Ii Jj

jacket   See page 122

ice cream   See page 119

On this page are pictures of words that begin with the letters "I" and "J". Can you find each word in your book? Turn to the page number you see near the picture. When you find the right word you will see this: ■

I

I have a bird and a turtle. **I'd** means "I had."
I'd not seen that TV program before. **I'll**
means "I will." **I'll** play with you tomorrow.
I'm means "I am." **I'm** going to the store with
my father. **I've** means "I have." **I've** been
home all day.

ice

Ice is something cold and hard. When water
freezes, it becomes **ice.** ■

ice cream

Ice cream is something to
eat. **Ice cream** is very cold. It
is sweet and tastes good. ■

ice-skate

Ice-skate means to move
along ice on **ice skates.** An
ice skate is a kind of shoe
with a long, sharp piece of
metal on the bottom.

idea

An **idea** is something that
you think of. Grandpa had a
good **idea** for what to put on
the snowman's head. ☼*See
the picture.*

Grandpa had a good **idea** for what
to put on the snowman's head.

if

If it rains, we will play inside. Ruth doesn't
know **if** she can go to the park with us.

important

When something is **important,** it means that it
matters very much. It is **important** that you
look both ways before you cross the road.

The hippopotamus is **in** the water.

in

Tom held the baby bird **in** his hand. Come **in** if it starts to rain. The hippopotamus is **in** the water. ☼*See the picture.*

inch

An **inch** is a word that is used to show how long something is. There are twelve **inches** in a foot.

indoor

Our school has an **indoor** swimming pool. The children went **indoors** when it began to rain.

insect

An **insect** is a very small animal. An **insect** has wings and three legs on each side of its body. Grasshoppers, ants, and mosquitoes are **insects.**

inside

The **inside** of our car is green. Joe looked **inside** the closet for his coat. The children played **inside** because it was raining. The owl is **inside** the tree. ☼*See the picture.*

The owl is **inside** the tree.

120

instead

Instead means that something is done in place of something else. We went to the playground after school **instead** of going right home.

into

Bill and Jim went **into** the house. The glass broke **into** pieces when Sharon dropped it. Joe put his hand **into** the bag to get a piece of candy. ☼*See the picture.*

iron

1. **Iron** is something very hard and strong. **Iron** is a metal. The bars of the tiger's cage were made of **iron.**
2. An **iron** is also a thing that is used to make clothes smooth. Mother is going to **iron** my dress for the party.

is

Betty **is** not at school today. Bill's coat **is** blue; Susan's **is** red. ☼*See the picture.* **Isn't** means "is not." This book **isn't** yours.

island

An **island** is a piece of land. There is water all around an **island.**

it

Tom threw the ball to Maria and she caught **it. It** is raining today. The cat cleaned **its** paws. **It's** means "it is" and "it has." **It's** cold outside today. **It's** been a long time since I've seen my friend Bob.

itch

When something makes you **itch,** you want to scratch it. The mosquito bite on John's arm **itched.**

Joe put his hand **into** the bag to get a piece of candy.

Bill's coat **is** blue; Susan's **is** red.

Ray was **jealous** because his friend had a new baseball glove.

jacket

A **jacket** is something to wear. It is a short coat. ■

jail

A **jail** is a place where someone who has broken a law has to stay. The policeman took the robber to **jail.**

jealous

You feel **jealous** when you are unhappy because someone has something that you do not have. Ray was **jealous** because his friend had a new baseball glove. ☼*See the picture.*

job

A **job** is something that has to be done. Suzanne's **job** was to feed the cat. My father has a **job** in an office.

join

Join means to put things together. The children **joined** hands. ☼*See the picture.*

The children **joined** hands.

joke

A **joke** is something that makes you laugh. John told a funny **joke** to the class. We hid Dad's shoes as a **joke.**

juice

Juice is something that you drink. You get **juice** from fruit by squeezing it. Orange **juice** is good to drink. You make lemonade with the **juice** of lemons.

jump

Jump means to go into the air. Alice had to **jump** to catch the ball. Michael **jumped** down from the tree. The fish **jumped** high out of the water. ☼*See the picture.* Tim made a big **jump** over the puddle.

The fish **jumped** high out of the water.

jungle

A **jungle** is a place that has a lot of trees and plants growing in it. It is very hot in a **jungle.** Monkeys live in **jungles.**

jury

A **jury** is a group of people. A **jury** decides whether someone has broken a law or not.

just

These shoes are **just** my size. Ted has **just** fed the dog. There was **just** one cookie left in the bag. ☼*See the picture.*

There was **just** one cookie left in the bag.

123

kangaroo   See page 125

Kk

key   See page 125

kitten   See page 127

On this page are pictures of words that begin with the letter "K". Can you find each word in your book? Turn to the page number you see near the picture. When you find the right word you will see this: ■

knife   See page 127

kangaroo

A **kangaroo** is an animal. A **kangaroo** has strong back legs that it uses for jumping. Mother **kangaroos** carry their babies in a pocket on their stomachs. ■

keep

Keep means to have something. Ted gave Ellen a kitten and her mother let her **keep** it. Peter **keeps** his toys in a box when he isn't playing with them. ☼*See the picture.* The teacher asked the children to **keep** quiet. The rain **kept** the children indoors.

Peter **keeps** his toys in a box when he isn't playing with them.

ketchup

Ketchup is something to put on food. It is made of tomatoes. I like to put **ketchup** on my hamburger.

key

A **key** is a small metal thing. You use a **key** to open or close a lock. Dad lost his **keys,** so he couldn't open the front door. ■

kick

Kick means to hit something with your foot. Joel **kicked** the ball down the field. ☼*See the picture.*

kid

Kid is a word we use when we are talking about a child. Jim said "Do you **kids** want to play baseball after school?"

kill

Kill means to make something die. The cat **killed** the mouse.

Joel **kicked** the ball down the field.

125

Ruth is a **kind** person who always tries to help other people.

kind

1. If someone is **kind** it means that they are nice. Ruth is a **kind** person who always tries to help other people. ☼*See the picture.*

2. **Kind** also means a group of things that are alike. Apples and oranges are **kinds** of fruit.

kindergarten

Kindergarten is a class in school. It comes before first grade.

king

A **king** is a man who rules a country. In the United States, we have a president instead of a **king.**

kiss

Kiss means to touch with your lips. You **kiss** someone to show that you love them. Dad always gives the children a **kiss** before he goes to work. ☼*See the picture.*

kitchen

A **kitchen** is a room where food is cooked. We have a stove and a refrigerator in our **kitchen.**

kite

A **kite** is something that you fly. **Kites** are made of paper. You fly a **kite** in the air at the end of a long string.

kitten

A **kitten** is a baby cat. ■

knee

The **knee** is a part of your body. Your **knee** is in the middle of your leg.

knife

A **knife** is something to cut with. A **knife** has a handle and a sharp piece of metal. ■

knock

Knock means to hit something. Jim **knocked** on the door. The puppy **knocked** the lamp off the table. ☼*See the picture.*

know

When you **know** something, it means that you are very sure about it. Kate **knows** all the children who live on her street. I wish I **knew** how to swim.

Dad always gives the children a **kiss** before he goes to work.

The puppy **knocked** the lamp off the table.

lamp   See page 129

ladder   See page 129

L l

lion   See page 137

On this page are pictures of words that begin with the letter "L". Can you find each word in your book? Turn to the page number you see near the picture. When you find the right word you will see this: ■

letter   See page 135

ladder

A **ladder** is something you can go up and down on. A **ladder** is a set of steps. Dad had to use a **ladder** so he could reach my kite that was caught in the tree. ■

lady

A **lady** is a woman. There is a **lady** on the telephone who wants to speak to Mom.

lake

A **lake** is water that has land all around it. We swim in the **lake** in the summer.

lamb

A **lamb** is a baby sheep.

lamp

A **lamp** is something that gives light. Sharon turned on the **lamp** in her room when it got dark outside. ■

land

Land is the part of the earth that we live on. The **land** around our house has lots of trees on it. The farmer grew corn on his **land**. The airplane **landed** at the airport. A cat always **lands** on its feet when it jumps. ☼*See the picture.*

A cat always **lands** on its feet when it jumps.

language

Language is words. We use **language** to speak to each other. English is the **language** that most people in the United States speak.

lap

You have a **lap** when you sit down. Your **lap** is between your waist and your knees. I sat on Mom's **lap** when she read me a story.

A tiger is a **large** animal.

large

Large means very big. A tiger is a **large** animal. ☼*See the picture.*

last

When something is **last**, it means that it comes at the end after everything else.

late

If you are **late** it means that you come after the time you are supposed to come. Sam was **late** for school this morning. ☼*See the picture.*

Sam was **late** for school this morning.

laugh

Laugh means to make sounds with your voice. You **laugh** when you are very happy or when you think that something is funny. We all **laughed** at the silly clowns at the circus. The baby always **laughs** when we make silly faces at her.

laundry

Laundry is clothes that need to be washed. Jack helped his mother put the **laundry** in the washing machine.

law

A **law** is something that tells you what you can do and what you cannot do. Our government makes **laws**. If someone drives a car too fast he is breaking the **law**. A **lawyer** is someone who knows a lot about **laws**. Our town has a **law** against throwing garbage in the lake.

lawn

A **lawn** is a place where grass grows. A **lawn** is around a house. My brother has to cut the **lawn** every Saturday.

lay

Lay means to put something down in a place. Mom **laid** the plates on the kitchen table for lunch. Hens **lay** eggs. Dad always **lays** his coat on the chair when he comes home from work.

lazy

If someone is **lazy** it means that they do not like to work. The **lazy** boy wouldn't clean up his room. My dog is **lazy** and just likes to sleep all day. ☼*See the picture.*

My dog is **lazy** and just likes to sleep all day.

The dog **leads** the man across the street.

lead

1. Lead means that you are first, ahead of other people. This word sounds like **seed**. The dog **leads** the man across the street. ☼*See the picture.* Lucy is the **leader** in the running race.
2. Lead is a part of a pencil. It is black. When you write with a pencil, you make the letters with the **lead**. This word sounds like **bed**.

leaf

A **leaf** is a part of a plant. **Leaves** are green and flat.

leak

When something **leaks**, it goes through a hole when it is not supposed to. The milk **leaked** from the paper cup all over the table.

learn

When you **learn** something it means that you get to know it for yourself. Laura **learned** to read this year. Carol is helping her brother **learn** how to swim. ☼*See the picture.*

Carol is helping her brother **learn** how to swim.

least

That boy does the **least** work of any of the children at school. The **least** you can do is help me clean up the room.

leave

When you **leave** a place, it means that you go away from it. We **leave** for school at eight o'clock in the morning. ☼*See the picture.* Did you **leave** your book at home again?

We **leave** for school at eight o'clock in the morning.

133

The boy is on the **left** side, and the girl is on the right.

left

1. Your body has a **left** side and a right side. In a car, the driver sits on the **left** side. In the picture, the boy is on the **left** side, and the girl is on the right.
2. We **left** the party early.

leg

Your leg is a part of your body. **Legs** are for standing on and walking. We have two **legs.** Animals have four **legs.** A chair has four **legs.**

lemon

A **lemon** is a yellow fruit. **Lemons** taste sour. You make **lemonade** with the juice of **lemons,** water, and sugar.

less

The black-and-white dog has **less** hair than the other one. ☼*See the picture.*

The black-and-white dog has **less** hair than the other one.

lesson

A **lesson** is something you learn. Tommy did well in the spelling **lesson** today. Sue is taking piano **lessons**.

let

If you **let** someone do something, it means
that you say that it is all right for them to do
it. Jean **lets** her brother ride her bicycle
sometimes. Dad **let** us stay up late last night.
Let's means "let us." **Let's** play ball.

letter

1. A **letter** is a part of the alphabet. A, B, and
C are **letters**. The word "bat" has three **letters**.
2. A **letter** is also something you write to
somebody. Joanne mailed the **letter** she wrote
to her grandmother thanking her for the
present. ■

library

A **library** is a place where books are kept.
Peter borrowed a book from the school
library.

lick

Lick means that you touch something with
your tongue. Betty **licked** her ice-cream cone.
The cat **licked** itself. ☼*See the picture.*

The cat **licked** itself.

lie

1. When you tell **lies** it means that you say
things that you know are not true. She was
telling a **lie** when she said she hadn't eaten
the last cookie, because she did. It is wrong to
lie to people.
2. **Lie** also means that you make yourself flat
on something. Sam likes to **lie** on the grass.
We **lie** in bed when we sleep.

life

If you have **life**, it means that you breathe
and grow. People and animals and plants have
life. A rock, a car, and a chair do not have **life**.

It was hard for Mike to **lift** the heavy bag.

lift

When you **lift** something it means that you pick it up. It was hard for Mike to **lift** the heavy bag. ☼*See the picture.*

light

Light is something that comes from the sun in the daytime. We can see things when we have **light**. Lamps and candles are **lights**. The lamp needs a new **light** bulb. Dad is going to **light** a fire so we can cook the hot dogs.

lightning

Lightning is a quick line of light that you see in the sky. There is **lightning** and thunder when there is a storm.

like

1. Alice looks **like** her brother. An airplane in the sky sometimes looks **like** a bird.
2. If you **like** something it means that it makes you happy. Jack **likes** to eat ice cream. ☼*See the picture.* June **liked** all the other children in her class.

Jack **likes** to eat ice cream.

line

A **line** is something that is long and thin. Susan drew a **line** on the paper with her pencil. The children stood in **line** while they waited for the bus.

lion

A **lion** is an animal. **Lions** are yellow and have a lot of fur around their necks. ■

lip

A **lip** is a part of your face. You have two **lips** around your mouth. When you kiss someone you use your **lips**.

liquid

A **liquid** is something that is wet when you touch it. A **liquid** can be poured from a bottle. Water and milk are **liquids**.

listen

When you **listen** to something you try to hear it in a careful way. Judy likes to **listen** to records on her record player. ☼*See the picture.*

Judy likes to **listen** to records on her record player.

That animal **lives** in a hole in the ground.

That bird has a **long** neck and **long** legs.

little

When something is **little** it is very small. My **little** sister can't walk yet. An ant is **little.**

live

Live means to breathe and grow. Some people **live** to be very old. Billy **lived** next door to me last year. That animal **lives** in a hole in the ground. ☼*See the picture.*

lock

A **lock** is a thing that holds something shut. You need a key to open a **lock**. Dad **locked** the door when we left the house.

long

When something is **long** it means that one end of it is far away from the other end. There is a **long** hall outside our classroom. That bird has a **long** neck and **long** legs. ☼*See the picture.* An hour is **longer** than a minute.

look

When you **look** at something you use your eyes to see it. Harry let me **look** at the pictures in his book. Grace is **looking** for her ball, but she hasn't found it. Roy **looked** happy when he saw his birthday cake.

loose

When something is **loose** it is going to come off soon. There is a **loose** button on my coat. Lee has a **loose** front tooth.

lose

When you **lose** something it means that you can't find it anywhere. Don't **lose** your new gloves. Jenny **lost** her pencil in the playground. Did Joe **lose** the swimming race?

lot

If there are a **lot** of things it means that there are many of them. There were a **lot** of birds on the ice. ☼*See the picture.* Mary ate **lots** of candy at the party.

There were a **lot** of birds on the ice.

loud

When something is **loud** it makes a lot of noise. The horns in the band are **loud.** Mom shouted **loudly** when she called us for dinner.

love

If you **love** someone, it means that you are very happy when you are with them. You hug and kiss someone you **love.** Grandpa **loves** his grandchildren. ☼*See the picture.*

low

When something is **low**, it means that it is close to the ground. The fence was **low** enough for me to jump over. I keep my toys on a **low** shelf.

lunch

Lunch is food. You eat **lunch** between breakfast and dinner. We take our **lunches** to school every day.

Grandpa **loves** his grandchildren.

139

monkey   See page 148

map   See page 143

M m

milk   See page 147

On this page are pictures of words that begin with the letter "M". Can you find each word in your book? Turn to the page number you see near the picture. When you find the right word you will see this: ■

mountain   See page 150

machine

A **machine** is a thing that does something. It has parts that move to make it work. Airplanes are **machines** that can fly. A washing **machine** is a **machine** that washes clothes.

mad

When you are **mad** it means that you are angry. Roger was **mad** at me for taking his crayons without asking him. Dad was **mad** when the car got a flat tire in the rain. ☼*See the picture.*

Dad was **mad** when the car got a flat tire in the rain.

made

The clown **made** us laugh.

magazine

A **magazine** is something to read. **Magazines** have stories and pictures.

magic

Magic is something that seems to be real but is not. The clown did **magic** tricks at the party. ☼*See the picture.* A **magician** is someone who does **magic** tricks.

mail

Letters and post cards are **mail**. **Mail** is sent through the post office. A **mailman** brings the **mail** to your house and puts it into a **mailbox**. Robert **mailed** a letter to his grandmother.

main

Main is a word you use when you want to show that something is the most important. The **main** parts of a clock are the hands that tell what time it is.

The clown did **magic** tricks at the party.

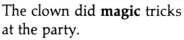

141

The children helped Dad **make** a house for the dog to sleep in.

make

Make means to cause something to happen. The children helped Dad **make** a house for the dog to sleep in. ☼*See the picture.* Funny stories always **make** him laugh. The smell of food cooking **makes** me hungry. Aunt Marie is **making** lunch for us.

make-believe

When something is **make-believe** it means that it is not real. Fairies are **make-believe**.

male

A **male** is a boy or man. Your father is a **male**.

man

A **man** is a grown-up male person.

We saw **many** different birds at the zoo.

many

Many is a word you use when you want to show that there are a lot of something. We saw **many** different birds at the zoo. ☼*See the picture.*

map

A **map** is a drawing that shows where different places are. ■

march

When people **march** together they all walk with the same steps. We **marched** in the parade on the Fourth of July.

mark

Mark means to make a spot on something. My dirty shoes **marked** the clean floor. The baby made **marks** on the wall with a crayon. ☼*See the picture.*

marry

Marry means to make someone your husband or wife.

The baby made **marks** on the wall with a crayon.

Ted's socks don't **match**
in color.

match

1. When things **match** it means that they are
like one another. Ted's socks don't **match** in
color. ☼*See the picture.*
2. A **match** is also a short piece of wood or
paper. When one end is rubbed against
something else it makes a flame.

matter

When someone asks you "What's the
matter?" they are asking you what is
bothering you. The doctor asked Ray what
was the **matter** with his foot.

may

It **may** rain this afternoon. ☼*See the picture.*

It **may** rain this afternoon.

maybe

Maybe it will snow tomorrow.

me

The bus takes **me** to school in the morning.

The whole family had a big **meal** on Thanksgiving.

meal

A **meal** is all the food you eat at one time. The whole family had a big **meal** on Thanksgiving. ☼*See the picture.*

mean

1. Someone who is **mean** is not nice. She was very **mean** to make fun of her sister.
2. Mean is also a word you use to show that two things are the same. The word "huge" **means** "big." "Be quiet" **means** "don't talk."
3. Mean is also a word you use to show what you are thinking. Mom really **meant** it when she told us to clean up our rooms.

meat

Meat is the part of an animal that we eat. Beef is **meat** from a cow. Bacon is **meat** from a pig.

medicine

Medicine is something we take when we are sick to make us feel better.

meet

Meet means to come together with someone. Timmy was happy to **meet** his sister's friend. ☼*See the picture.* Dave **met** me in the park.

Timmy was happy to **meet** his sister's friend.

men

Men means more than one man. Two **men** came to fix the television set.

mess

When something is a **mess**, it means that it is dirty and the things in it are not where they are supposed to be. The room was a **mess** with toys lying all over the floor.

metal

Metal is something that is very hard and strong. It is found in the earth. Iron is a **metal**.

mice

Mice means more than one mouse.

middle

The **middle** is the part that is in the center. In the picture below, the baby animal is in the **middle**.

The baby animal is in the **middle**.

might

We **might** be late for school if we don't hurry.

milk

Milk is something to drink. It is white and comes from cows. You put **milk** on cereal. Sue **milks** the cows on her farm every morning. ☼*See the picture.* ■

mind

1. The **mind** is the part of you that thinks and feels things. You use your **mind** to learn and remember things.
2. Mind also means to do what someone asks you to do. "**Mind** your mother," my father said, "and clean up your room now."

mine

That book is yours; this one is **mine**.

minute

A **minute** is a part of an hour. There are sixty **minutes** in an hour.

miss

1. Miss means to not get something. If Dad doesn't hurry he will **miss** the train. Joe **missed** the ball. ☼*See the picture.*
2. Miss also means to be sorry that someone you like is not with you. I will **miss** my older sister when she goes to camp this summer.

mistake

A **mistake** is something that is wrong. I made two **mistakes** in spelling on the test.

Sue **milks** the cows on her farm every morning.

Joe **missed** the ball.

mitten

A **mitten** is something you wear on your hand. We wear **mittens** when it is cold.

mix

Mix means to put different things together. Grandmother **mixed** lemon juice, water, and sugar to make lemonade. ☼*See the picture.*

Grandmother **mixed** lemon juice, water, and sugar to make lemonade.

mom

Mom is a name for your mother. Some children also call their mother **Mommy**.

money

Money is what you use to buy something with. Nickels, dimes, and dollars are **money**.

monkey

A **monkey** is an animal. It has long arms and legs. **Monkeys** use their hands and feet to climb trees. ■

month

A **month** is a part of a year. There are twelve **months** in a year. The **months** are January, February, March, April, May, June, July, August, September, October, November, and December.

moon

The **moon** is the yellow thing that shines in the sky at night. The **moon** goes around the earth.

more

The number four is three **more** than one. Do you want any **more** milk? Ellen picked **more** flowers than the other children. ☼*See the picture.*

Ellen picked **more** flowers than the other children.

morning

Morning is the first part of the day.

mosquito

A **mosquito** is a small insect. **Mosquitoes** bite you and make you want to scratch.

most

Most of the kittens were sleeping. ☼*See the picture.*

mother

Your **mother** is one of your parents. Your **mother** is a woman.

motor

A **motor** is a thing that makes a machine work. The **motor** of a car makes it go.

Most of the kittens were sleeping.

mountain

A **mountain** is a very high piece of land. A **mountain** is much higher than a hill. ■

mouse

A **mouse** is a small animal. It has a long, thin tail.

mouth

The **mouth** is an open place on your face. You put food into your **mouth**. Words and sounds come out of your **mouth**. Your tongue and teeth are in your **mouth**.

move

Move means to go from one place to another. We helped Mom **move** the box from the floor to the table. We **moved** closer to the teacher so we could hear better. Our family is going to **move** to a new house. ☼*See the picture.*

Our family is going to **move** to a new house.

movie

A **movie** is pictures that move. We went to see a **movie** about cowboys on Saturday.

much

Much is a word that you use to show that there is a lot of something. Dad had so **much** work that he had to stay late at the office. ☼*See the picture.* We had too **much** rain this week.

mud

Mud is wet dirt. We got **mud** all over the kitchen floor when we came in from the rain.

multiply

Multiply means to make a number bigger. When we **multiply** we add a number to itself many times. If you **multiply** 2 times 4, you add 2 to itself 4 times.

muscle

A **muscle** is something that helps you move the parts of your body. **Muscles** help you to lift and carry heavy things.

music

The sounds made by a piano, guitar, or violin are **music**. **Music** is nice to listen to. Our teacher played some **music** on the piano and we all sang a song.

must

Dad said I **must** clean up my room before I can go out to play. ☼*See the picture.*

my

Alan is **my** brother. That is **my** pencil. I baked these cookies **myself**. I cut **myself** with the scissors.

Dad had so **much** work that he had to stay late at the office.

Dad said I **must** clean up my room before I can go out to play.

151

orange   See page 160

nest   See page 155

Nn

Oo

newspaper   See page 156

ocean   See page 158

On this page are pictures of words that begin with the letters "N" and "O". Can you find each word in your book? Turn to the page number you see near the picture. When you find the right word you will see this: ■

nail

1. A **nail** is a thin piece of metal. It is pointed at one end and flat at the other. You can hammer **nails** into two pieces of wood to hold them together. Dad **nailed** the picture to the wall.

2. A **nail** is also the hard part on the ends of your fingers and toes.

name

A **name** is a word that you call something by. My friend's **name** is Debbie Taylor. *Oak* and *pine* are the **names** of two kinds of trees. *Chicago* is the **name** of a big city. We **named** our new kitten "Boots."

nap

A **nap** is a short sleep. The baby takes a **nap** in the afternoon. Mom took a **nap** while the children were out playing with Dad. ☼*See the picture.*

napkin

A **napkin** is something you use to clean your mouth and fingers when you are eating. We took paper **napkins** to the picnic.

Mom took a **nap** while the children were out playing with Dad.

nature

Nature is all the things that are not made by people. Mountains, trees, rivers, and the ocean are parts of **nature**. All animals are also parts of **nature.**

153

The pigs were standing **near** the fence.

near

When something is **near** it means that it is not far away. My grandparents live in a house **near** ours. The pigs were standing **near** the fence. ☼*See the picture.*

neat

When something is **neat**, it means that it is clean and that everything is where it is supposed to be. My sister always has a **neat** room.

neck

Your **neck** is a part of your body. It is between your head and your shoulders. Ann wore a pretty chain around her **neck**. A camel has a long **neck**.

need

Need means to have to have something. The dog **needs** to be fed every day. You will **need** a sweater if you are going outdoors. Bobby **needed** a new pair of sneakers. ☼*See the picture.*

needle

A **needle** is a thin piece of metal. **Needles** have a hole in one end. Mother uses a **needle** and thread to sew. The doctor put the **needle** in John's arm when he gave him a shot.

Bobby **needed** a new pair of sneakers.

neighbor

A **neighbor** is someone who lives near you. Our **neighbor** took care of our dog when we went away on vacation.

neither

Neither of the puppies was the same color as its mother. ☼*See the picture.* Jim doesn't want to go to the movies, and **neither** does his brother. **Neither** Jerry nor Ralph won the race.

Neither of the puppies was the same color as its mother.

nest

A **nest** is something a bird builds to live in. Birds lay their eggs in **nests**. ■

never

Mike has **never** been to the circus. You **never** told me that you had a baby sister. I **never** saw such a beautiful doll before.

new

When something is **new** it means that it has never been used before. We bought a **new** television set when our old one broke. ☼*See the picture.*

news

News is the story of something that has happened. We watched the day's **news** on television last night. Did you read the **news** in the newspaper yesterday about the fire at school?

We bought a **new** television set when our old one broke.

newspaper

A newspaper is something to read. It is made of sheets of paper that are folded together. **Newspapers** tell you about things that have happened. ■

next

Bill is going to camp **next** week. Barbara is the **next** person in line. The baby deer stayed **next** to its mother. ☼*See the picture.*

The baby deer stayed **next** to its mother.

nice

When something is **nice** it makes you happy. The sun was shining, and it was a **nice** day. It was **nice** of Julie to let us use her bicycle.

nickel

A **nickel** is a piece of money. It is made of metal. A **nickel** is the same thing as five pennies.

night

Night is the time when it is dark outside. The baby slept all through the **night**. Friday is the **night** of the basketball game.

no

No, I don't want any ice cream. Mom said **no** when I asked to stay up late. There was **no** mail in the mailbox. ☼*See the picture.*

nobody

I knocked on the door, but **nobody** answered.

noise

A **noise** is a loud sound. The airplane made a lot of **noise** when it took off. We were so **noisy** that mother asked us to go outside to play.

There was **no** mail in the mailbox.

156

none

None of us could climb as high as Jill.

noon

Noon means the same thing as twelve o'clock in the daytime. We ate our lunch at **noon**.

north

When you look at a map, the top part is **north**. If you face the sun when it comes up in the morning, **north** is on your left.

nose

Your **nose** is a part of your face. It sticks out from the middle of your face. You breathe and smell things through your **nose**.

not

Alex is **not** at school today. Our cat does **not** like to go swimming. ☼*See the picture.*

Our cat does **not** like to go swimming.

nothing

Dave wanted some candy, but there was **nothing** left in the box. ☼*See the picture.*

now

Do you really have to go **now**? Lee should be home by **now**. It is snowing **now**.

number

A **number** tells you how many there are of something. *2* and *50* are **numbers**. The **number** of children in our family is three. Do you know your own telephone **number**? The pages in this book are **numbered**.

nut

A **nut** is something to eat. **Nuts** come from plants. **Nuts** have hard shells on the outside.

Dave wanted some candy, but there was **nothing** left in the box.

Sue jumped **off** the dock into the water.

ocean

The **ocean** is salt water. It covers large parts of the earth. Fish live in the **ocean**. Big ships sail on the **ocean**. ■

o'clock

O'clock is a word that you use when you say what time it is. We go to school at eight **o'clock** in the morning.

of

The color **of** my dress is red. My doll house is made **of** wood.

off

Sally took a dish **off** the shelf. Sue jumped **off** the dock into the water. ☼*See the picture.* Take **off** your coat. Please turn the TV **off**.

office

An **office** is a place where work is done. Dad goes to his **office** every morning. We went to the doctor's **office** when I was sick.

often

If you do something **often**, you do it many times. We went to the beach **often** during the summer. Timmy **often** builds model cars. ☼*See the picture.*

Timmy **often** builds model cars.

OK

When you say **OK**, you mean that something is all right. Is it **OK** if I borrow your bicycle?

old

When you say someone is **old** it means that they have lived for a long time. My grandfather is **old**. I am five years **old.**

on

The bird is sitting **on** the fence. ☼*See the picture.* We went to the circus **on** Saturday. Karen put her boots **on**. The radio is **on**.

The bird is sitting **on** the fence.

once

If you do something **once** you do it one time. We buy groceries **once** a week. I saw an elephant **once** in a zoo. **Once** it stops raining we can go outdoors.

one

One is the smallest number of anything that you can have. There is only **one** cookie left.

only

Only Carol can run faster than me. There was **only** one sheep in the field. ☼*See the picture.*

open

When something is **open** it means that you can get in or out of it. Joan walked through the **open** door of the house. Jack **opened** the birthday present. School will **open** soon.

There was **only** one sheep in the field.

159

Carol and Betty sat **opposite** each other at the table.

opposite

When something is **opposite** you, it is right across from you. There is a playground **opposite** my school. Carol and Betty sat **opposite** each other at the table. ☼*See the picture.*

or

Do you want ice cream **or** cake for dessert?

orange

An **orange** is something to eat. It is a small, round fruit. We like to drink **orange** juice for breakfast. ■

other

I want to wear my **other** dress to the party. Do you have any **other** toys? Jimmy put on one shoe, but he couldn't find the **other**. ☼*See the picture.*

our

Our house is near school. That white dog is **ours**.

Jimmy put on one shoe, but he couldn't find the **other**.

out

Tom took the toy **out** of the box. The children couldn't go **out** to play, because it was too cold. Please turn **out** the light.

outdoor

Baseball is an **outdoor** game. We had a picnic **outdoors** in the park.

outside

The **outside** of our house is painted white. The boys went **outside** to play in the yard. ☼*See the picture.*

oven

An **oven** is a thing to cook in. An **oven** is part of a stove. Mother is baking cookies in the **oven**.

over

The fox jumped **over** the log. ☼*See the picture.* Mother put a blanket **over** the bed. School is **over** for the summer. Joan did her drawing **over**. The cat knocked the lamp **over**.

The boys went **outside** to play in the yard.

The fox jumped **over** the log.

owl

An **owl** is a bird. It has a round head and large eyes. **Owls** fly around at night.

own

When you **own** something you have it to keep. I **own** a bicycle. This book is my **own**, but that one is my sister's.

161

pumpkin   See page 179

Pp Qq

queen   See page 181

piano   See page 169

On this page are pictures of words that begin with the letters "P" and "Q". Can you find each word in your book? Turn to the page number you see near the picture. When you find the right word you will see this: ■

pack

Pack means to fill up something with other things. Dad **packed** his suitcase when he went on a trip. ☼*See the picture.* We **packed** all my toys in boxes when we moved to a new house.

package

A **package** is a box with something in it. We sent a **package** of cookies to my sister at camp. There were lots of pretty **packages** under the Christmas tree.

page

A **page** is one side of a piece of paper. Books, newspapers, and magazines have **pages.** Nancy wrote her name on the first **page** of her school book.

Dad **packed** his suitcase when he went on a trip.

pail

A **pail** is a thing to hold something in. A **pail** has a handle. Mom bought my little sister a new **pail** to put sand in when we go to the beach.

pain

A **pain** is where you hurt. Jack had a **pain** in his elbow when he hit it against the table.

paint

Paint is something that is used to color things. **Paint** is wet like water, but it dries when you put it on something. The **paint** on the outside of our house is white. Dad **painted** the fence green.

pair

A **pair** is two things that go together. My brother Bobby has a new **pair** of ice skates. ☼*See the picture.*

pajamas

Pajamas are something to wear when you go to sleep. **Pajamas** are a shirt and a pair of pants.

pan

A **pan** is a thing to cook in. Mother cooked the bacon in the frying **pan**. We baked the cake in a **pan**.

pancake

A **pancake** is something to eat. It is flat and thin. I like to put butter on my **pancakes**.

pants

Pants are something you wear to cover your legs. **Pants** have two parts, and each part covers one leg. Jamie ripped his **pants** climbing over the fence.

My brother Bobby has a new **pair** of ice skates.

paper

Paper is something you use to write on. Books have pages made of **paper**. We wrap presents in pretty colored **paper**. The teacher gave each of us a piece of **paper** to write our names on.

parade

A **parade** is a lot of people walking together. Bands play music in **parades**. The children watched the **parade** of animals at the circus.

parakeet

A **parakeet** is a bird. It has a long, pointed tail and very pretty feathers.

parent

A **parent** is a mother or a father. Your mother and father are your **parents**.

park

1. A **park** is a piece of land with trees and grass. **Parks** have playgrounds and places for sitting. My grandfather takes us to the **park**.
2. **Park** also means to put something in a place where it can stay for a while. Dad **parked** the car in front of the house.

part

A **part** is a piece of something. I think dessert is the best **part** of dinner. Your head is a **part** of your body. A television set is made of many **parts**. Linda played the **part** of the queen in the school play.

party

A **party** is a lot of people who are having a good time together. Each child brought a present to the **party**. ☼*See the picture.*

Each child brought a present to the **party**.

pass

Pass means to go by. We **pass** your house on the way to school. Please **pass** me the salt.

past

When something is **past** it means that it has gone by. It has rained for the **past** two days. Jack threw the ball **past** the catcher.

paste

Paste is something that is used to make things stick together. Charles **pasted** the pictures of animals in a book.

pat

Pat means to touch something softly with your hand. My dog wags his tail when I **pat** him. ☼*See the picture.*

My dog wags his tail when I **pat** him.

path

A **path** is something that you walk on. We walked in the woods on a **path** that led to a lake. Dad shoveled a **path** through the snow from the road to our front door.

patient

When you are **patient**, it means that you can wait for something quietly. Mother told us to be **patient** when we asked what time we were leaving for the zoo.

pattern

A **pattern** is the way colors and lines look on a thing. Julie's dress had a pretty flower **pattern** on it.

paw

A **paw** is the foot of an animal. Dogs and cats have **paws**.

pay

Pay means to give money to someone for something. Dad **paid** the man ten dollars for putting gas in the car. ☼*See the picture.*

pea

A **pea** is something to eat. A **pea** is a vegetable.

peace

Peace means a time when there is no fighting. When the world is at **peace**, there are no wars.

peach

A **peach** is something sweet to eat. A **peach** is a fruit.

peanut

A **peanut** is something to eat. It has a shell. **Peanuts** grow under the ground. **Peanut butter** is a soft food that is made from peanuts.

pear

A **pear** is something to eat. A **pear** is a fruit.

pebble

A **pebble** is a small stone.

peek

Peek means to look at something quickly. Eddie **peeked** into the box. ☼*See the picture.*

pen

A **pen** is a thing to write with.

Dad **paid** the man ten dollars for putting gas in the car.

Eddie **peeked** into the box.

167

Jane's spelling test was **perfect**.

pencil
A **pencil** is a thing to write with. It is a long stick of wood with lead in it.

penny
A **penny** is a piece of money. **Pennies** are made of metal. A **penny** is the same thing as a **cent**.

people
Men, women, and children are **people**. There were twenty **people** at my party.

pepper
Pepper is something to put on food. It is used to make food taste better. **Pepper** can burn your mouth when you taste it.

perfect
When something is **perfect**, it means that there is nothing wrong with it. Jane's spelling test was **perfect**. ☼*See the picture.*

perhaps
Perhaps means that something may happen. **Perhaps** it will rain this afternoon.

period
A **period** is a small dot at the end of a sentence.

person
A **person** is a man, woman, or child. There was only one **person** waiting for the bus.

pet
A **pet** is an animal that you have in your home. Dogs, cats, and birds are **pets**. Joe has two **pet** rabbits. ☼*See the picture.*

Joe has two **pet** rabbits.

phone

A **phone** is a thing that you use when you talk to someone who is far away from you. A **phone** has wires that carry the sound of your voice. A **phone** is the same thing as a **telephone**. We are going to **phone** my aunt and uncle tonight to find out when they are coming to visit us.

piano

A **piano** is a thing that makes music when you play it. You play the **piano** with your fingers. ■

pick

1. Pick means to take up something with your fingers. We **picked** some flowers for Mother's birthday. The children had to **pick** up their toys when they were finished playing. ☼*See the picture.*
2. Pick also means to choose something. Mom let me **pick** out a new dress at the store.

picnic

When you go on a **picnic** you take food with you and eat it outdoors. Mom made sandwiches and we all went to the beach for a **picnic**.

The children had to **pick** up their toys when they were finished playing.

picture

1. A **picture** is something that you draw or paint. Carol drew a **picture** of a tree.
2. A **picture** is also something you see on television or at the movies.

Ron had a **piece** of cake for lunch.

Mary **pinned** a flower to her coat.

pie

A **pie** is something to eat. Some **pies** are sweet and have fruit in them.

piece

A **piece** is a part of something. Ron had a **piece** of cake for lunch. ☼*See the picture.* The teacher gave each child a **piece** of paper.

pig

A **pig** is an animal. It has a fat body, short legs, and a short tail.

pile

A **pile** is a lot of things lying one on top of the other. The girls raked all the leaves into a big **pile**. Dad cut the wood and **piled** it up in back of the house.

pill

A **pill** is something to take when you are sick. It is a small piece of medicine.

pillow

A **pillow** is a thing to put under your head when you sleep. **Pillows** are soft.

pilot

A **pilot** is someone who flies an airplane.

pin

A **pin** is a thing that is used to hold things together. It is a piece of metal with a point at one end. Mary **pinned** a flower to her coat. ☼*See the picture.*

pipe

A **pipe** is a thing that carries water. The water in a house goes through **pipes**.

pitch

Pitch means to throw something. Bob can **pitch** a ball very fast. ☼*See the picture.* Gail is going to be the **pitcher** for our team.

place

A **place** is where something is. Here is a **place** to hang your coat. Our town is a nice **place** to live.

plan

Plan means to think out a way to do something ahead of time. What time do you **plan** to go to the playground? Has your family made any **plans** for where you will go for your vacation?

plane

A **plane** is a thing that can fly in the air. It has two wings and an engine to make it go. A **plane** is the same thing as an **airplane**.

planet

A **planet** is a very large thing in the sky that goes around the sun. The earth is a **planet**.

plant

A **plant** is any living thing that is not an animal. Trees, flowers, and grass are **plants**. Grandpa **planted** a tree in the back yard. ☼*See the picture.*

plate

A **plate** is a thing to put food on. **Plates** are round and flat.

Bob can **pitch** a ball very fast.

Grandpa **planted** a tree in the back yard.

171

play

1. **Play** means to do something for fun. The dog **played** with the ball.

2. A **play** is also a story that you act in. Our class is going to give a Christmas **play** for our parents.

3. **Play** also means to make music on a thing. Jeff knows how to **play** the piano.

playground

A **playground** is a place where you can play outdoors. Some **playgrounds** have swings.

please

Please is a word that you use when you ask for something in a nice way.

plenty

Plenty means that there is a lot of something. There was **plenty** of corn for everybody at the picnic. ☼*See the picture.*

There was **plenty** of corn for everybody at the picnic.

plus

Two **plus** two is four.

pocket

A **pocket** is a place in your clothes to put things. Dan put the pencil in the **pocket** of his pants.

pocketbook

A **pocketbook** is a thing that a girl or woman carries small things in.

poem

A **poem** is a kind of writing that uses words in a special way. **Poems** are nice to read.

point

1. A **point** is the sharp end of something. Needles and pins have **points**.
2. **Point** also means to use your finger to show where something is. The policeman **pointed** to show us which road to take to the beach.
☼*See the picture.*

The policeman **pointed** to show us which road to take to the beach.

poison

Poison is something that can hurt or kill living things. When my mother cleans the kitchen floor, she uses something that is **poison** if you drink it.

pole

A **pole** is a long piece of wood. The flag flies from a **pole** in front of our school. Norm got a new fishing **pole** for his birthday.

police

The **police** are a group of people who work to keep us safe. The **police** also make sure that people don't break the laws. The **police** arrested the man who stole the money and put him in jail. A **policeman** is a man who works for the **police**. A **policewoman** is a woman who works for the **police**.

polite

When someone is **polite**, it means that they are nice to others. Peter is a **polite** boy who always tries to help people. ☼*See the picture.*

pollute

Pollute means to make something dirty. If garbage is thrown into a river it will **pollute** the river. Smoke from automobiles causes **pollution** of the air.

pond

A **pond** is water with land all around it. It is smaller than a lake. The **pond** in back of our house has fish and frogs in it.

pony

A **pony** is a small horse. My sister and I rode the **ponies** at the fair.

Peter is a **polite** boy who always tries to help people.

pool

A **pool** is a thing that has water in it to swim in. Our school has a **pool** indoors. There is a big outdoor **pool** in the park where we go swimming in the summer.

poor

When someone is **poor**, they have very little money. The girl in the story was **poor** until she grew up and married the rich prince.

pop

Pop means to make a short, loud noise. Jimmy's balloon **popped** when he held it too tightly. ☼*See the picture.* The firecracker went off with a **pop**.

popcorn

Popcorn is something good to eat. It is a kind of corn that opens with a pop when you cook it.

porch

A **porch** is a part of a house that is outdoors. It is covered by a roof. We sit on the **porch** in the summer.

pot

A **pot** is a thing to cook in. **Pots** have handles. Mom makes soup in a big **pot**.

potato

A **potato** is something to eat. **Potatoes** grow under the ground. A **potato** is a vegetable.

pound

A **pound** is a word that we use to show how much something weighs. My baby brother weighed eight **pounds** when he was born.

Jimmy's balloon **popped** when he held it too tightly.

Dad **poured** a glass of juice
for each of the children.

pour
Pour means to make a liquid go from one
place to another. Dad **poured** a glass of juice
for each of the children. ☼*See the picture.*

pray
When you **pray**, you speak to God.

present
A **present** is something that you give to
someone. There were many **presents** under
the Christmas tree.

president
A **president** is someone who is the leader of a
group of people. The **President** of the United
States·is the leader of the government.

pretend
When you **pretend**, you make believe you are
doing something. Joel **pretended** to be asleep
when his mother called him. Larry and Joan
pretended to be a king and queen. ☼*See the
picture.*

Larry and Joan **pretended**
to be a king and queen.

176

pretty
When something is **pretty**, it is nice to look at. Flowers are **pretty.**

prince
A **prince** is the son of a king or queen. A **princess** is the daughter of a king or queen.

principal
A **principal** is someone who is the leader of a school. Mrs. Jones is our school **principal**.

print
Print means to write in letters like the letters in a book. The teacher **printed** her name on the blackboard. ☼*See the picture.*

prison
A **prison** is a place where someone who has broken a law has to stay. The policemen took the man who robbed the bank to **prison**.

prize
A **prize** is something that you win for doing something the best. Janice won the **prize** for being first in the race.

probably
We will **probably** go to the beach on Saturday. Dad will **probably** be home soon.

problem
A **problem** is something that is hard to answer. There were ten **problems** on the arithmetic test.

program
A **program** is a show that you watch on television.

The teacher **printed** her name on the blackboard.

promise

Promise means to say that you will do something for sure. Rick **promised** to come home right after school. Betsy gave her mother a **promise** that she would clean her room right away.

property

Property is anything that someone owns. Bob's bicycle is his **property**. The playground is on school **property**.

protect

Protect means to keep someone from getting hurt. The police **protect** the people in our town. Football players wear special hats to **protect** their heads.

proud

When someone is **proud**, it means that they feel good about something that they have done. Ron was very **proud** of the card he made for his mother for Valentine's Day. ☼*See the picture.*

Ron was very **proud** of the card he made for his mother for Valentine's Day.

prove

Prove means to show that something is true. I can **prove** that this book is mine because it has my name on it.

public

If something is **public**, it means that it is for all people. A **public** school is a school for everyone. A **public** beach is for anybody to use.

pudding

Pudding is something to eat. It is soft and sweet. We had chocolate **pudding** for dessert.

The dogs **pulled** the sled across the snow.

pull

Pull means to hold something and move it toward you. The dogs **pulled** the sled across the snow. ☼*See the picture.*

pumpkin

A **pumpkin** is a fruit. It is big and round and has an orange skin. ■

punch

Punch means to hit someone hard with your fist. Jack **punched** Timmy on the arm when they had a fight.

punish

Punish is to make somebody know they have done something wrong. Dad **punished** the dog for chewing up his shoe. ☼*See the picture.*

pupil

A **pupil** is someone who goes to school.

Dad **punished** the dog for chewing up his shoe.

179

puppy

A **puppy** is a baby dog. Our dog had six **puppies** last week.

purpose

When you do something on **purpose**, it means that you mean to do it. Chuck did not break the cup on **purpose**; it slipped out of his hand.

purse

A **purse** is a thing that a girl or woman carries small things in. A **purse** is the same thing as a **pocketbook**. Mom put her keys into her **purse**.

push

Push means to use your hand to move something. You have to **push** hard to make that door open. Karen **pushed** the shopping cart for her mother. Betty gave her brother a **push** that almost made him fall down.

put

Put means to make something be in a place. I **put** the plates on the table. Kevin **put** his cap on his head. Jane **put** the flowers in the vase. ☼*See the picture.*

Jane **put** the flowers in the vase.

quart

A **quart** is a word that we use to show how much of something there is. Dad bought three **quarts** of milk at the store.

quarter

A quarter is a piece of money. It is made of metal. A **quarter** is the same as twenty-five cents. Four **quarters** make one dollar.

queen

A **queen** is a woman who rules a country. ■

queer

When something is **queer**, it means that there is something strange about it. Lucy painted a **queer** animal with blue fur and green legs.

Beth knew the answer to the teacher's **question**.

question

When you ask a **question**, you are trying to find out something. Beth knew the answer to the teacher's **question**. ☼*See the picture.*

quick

When something is **quick**, it means that it is done very fast. The mouse ran **quickly** into the hole. ☼*See the picture.*

quiet

When you are **quiet**, it means that you are not making any noise. The children were all **quiet** while the teacher read them a story.

quite

My grandmother is **quite** old. It is not **quite** time for dinner.

The mouse ran **quickly** into the hole.

rabbit   See page 183

rose   See page 190

radio   See page 183

On this page are pictures of words that begin with the letter "R". Can you find each word in your book? Turn to the page number you see near the picture. When you find the right word you will see this: ■

rabbit

A **rabbit** is a small animal. It has long ears and a small tail. **Rabbits** hop very fast. ■

race

You have a **race** to find out who can go the fastest. Donna won the **race** because she is the best runner. The horses **raced** around the track.

radio

A **radio** is a thing you can turn on and listen to. We hear music on the **radio**. ■

railroad

A **railroad** is a road that trains go on. It has long, metal pieces that the wheels of the trains run on.

rain

Rain is drops of water that come down from the sky. Donny got caught in the **rain** without his umbrella. We couldn't have a picnic because it **rained.**

raincoat

A **raincoat** is something that you wear to keep dry in the rain.

raise

When you **raise** something it means that you lift it up. Karen **raised** her hand because she knew the answer to the teacher's question. Carl and Alice helped the teacher **raise** the flag. ☼*See the picture.* The farmer **raises** corn in his field.

Carl and Alice helped the teacher **raise** the flag.

The deer **ran** quickly into the woods when it saw us coming.

Jennifer **rang** the doorbell.

ran

The deer **ran** quickly into the woods when it saw us coming. ☼*See the picture.*

ranch

A **ranch** is a kind of large farm. There are cows, sheep, and horses on a **ranch**.

rang

Jennifer **rang** the doorbell. ☼*See the picture.*

rat

A **rat** is an animal. It looks like a large mouse. **Rats** have long, thin tails.

rather

Jack would **rather** have ice cream than cake for dessert.

reach

When you **reach** something, you put out your hand to touch it. Mary can't **reach** the top shelf in her closet unless she stands on her toes. Joe **reached** up to catch the ball. ☼*See the picture.*

read

When you know how to **read**, you can look at words and know what they mean. The children are learning to **read** at school.

ready

When you are **ready**, it means that you have all the things you need to do something. When all our clothes were packed and everybody was in the car, we were **ready** to go on our trip. The boys were **ready** to start the race. ☼*See the picture.*

Joe **reached** up to catch the ball.

real

When something is **real**, you know it is true. Is that a **real** bug or a rubber one? The giant in the fairy tale was not **real**.

really

You use the word **really** to show that you are very sure about something. I **really** want to be a doctor when I grow up. We had a **really** good time at the circus.

reason

A **reason** is something that tells you why something happened. What was Ellen's **reason** for being late?

The boys were **ready** to start the race.

recess

A **recess** is a time when you stop work. The children played outside during **recess**.

record

A **record** is a thing that can make music. It is round and flat. You play a **record** on a special machine. Susie has a **record** of pretty songs.

refrigerator

A **refrigerator** is a thing you put food in to keep it cold.

relax

When you **relax** it means that you are not doing anything for a while. Dad likes to **relax** when he comes home from work. ☼*See the picture.*

Dad likes to **relax** when he comes home from work.

remember

When you **remember** something, it means that you think of it again. Do you **remember** what you did last summer? Jim **remembered** to bring his books home from school.

rest

1. When you **rest**, you stop what you are doing for a little while. The children **rested** because they were tired from running around. We have a short **rest** at school in the morning.
2. Rest also means something that is left after everything else is gone. I ate the **rest** of the cake after the birthday party was over.

restaurant

A **restaurant** is a place to eat. Someone brings food to your table and you pay for it.

return

When you **return** something you give it back. Jane **returned** the book to the library. ☼*See the picture.*

ribbon

A **ribbon** is a long piece of cloth. Sue has a yellow **ribbon** in her hair.

rice

Rice is something to eat. **Rice** is the little white parts of a plant. We had chicken soup with **rice.**

rich

If you are **rich**, you have a lot of money. The king in the story was very **rich**.

ride

When you **ride** something, you sit on it and move. Helen likes to **ride** her bicycle in the park. ☼*See the picture.* Mom **rides** to work in a bus. The cowboy **rode** a horse.

Jane **returned** the book to the library.

Helen likes to **ride** her bicycle in the park.

187

The baby animal is on the **right**.

right

1. Your body has a left side and a **right** side. People drive cars on the **right** side of the road. In the picture above, the baby animal is on the **right**.

2. Right also means that something has no mistakes in it. Nancy gave the **right** answer to the teacher's question.

ring

1. A **ring** is something round. Mom wears a **ring** on her finger.

2. Ring also means to make a sound like a bell. Did you hear the telephone **ring**?

river

A **river** is water that has land on both sides.

road

A **road** is a way of going from one place to another. Cars go on **roads**.

roast

Roast means to cook in a stove or over a fire. The children **roasted** hot dogs over the fire. ☼*See the picture.*

rob

Rob means to take something that does not belong to you. The man **robbed** the bank. The police are looking for the **robber** who took the money from the bank.

rock

A **rock** is something that is very hard. **Rocks** are found on the ground. The children climbed over the **rocks** in the park.

roll

1. Roll means to move by turning over and over. The ball **rolled** off the table. One of the baby bears **rolled** on his back. ☼*See the picture.*
2. A **roll** is also a small piece of bread. Jill put the hot dog on a **roll**.

roller skate

A **roller skate** is a thing that you put on your shoe. **Roller skates** have four wheels on the bottom. Fred likes to **roller-skate** on the sidewalk in front of his house.

roof

A **roof** is the top of a house.

room

A **room** is a part of a house. Your **room** is where you sleep and keep all your clothes and your toys.

The children **roasted** hot dogs over the fire.

One of the baby bears **rolled** on his back.

189

rooster

A **rooster** is a male chicken.

root

A **root** is a part of a plant. **Roots** grow under the ground.

rope

Rope is a kind of thick string. Our swing hangs from the tree on **ropes**.

rose

A **rose** is a flower. **Roses** smell good. **Roses** can be red, white, or yellow. ■

rough

When something is **rough**, it means that it is full of bumps. The bark of a tree feels **rough** when you touch it. Mom told us not to be so **rough** when we played or we might get hurt. The ocean was **rough** during the storm. ☼*See the picture.*

The ocean was **rough** during the storm.

round

When something is **round**, it looks like a ball.

row

A **row** is things or people in a line. My desk is in the last **row** in our classroom.

rub

When you **rub** something, you touch it and move your hand over it. The cat **rubbed** against Tom's leg. ☼*See the picture.*

rubber

Rubber is something that you can pull and it won't break. My ball is made of **rubber**. The eraser at the end of my pencil is made of **rubber**. Harry wore **rubbers** over his shoes to keep his feet dry in the rain.

rude

When you are **rude**, you are not being nice to someone. It was **rude** of Tom to yell at Ellen when she asked to borrow his book.

rug

A **rug** is something that covers a floor.

rule

A **rule** is something that tells you what you can do and what you cannot do. One of the **rules** at school is that you cannot run in the halls. Baseball, football, and other games have **rules.**

run

Run means to move as fast as you can. The children had to **run** to catch the bus. Elsie was the best **runner** in the race. The man at the garage fixed our car so it would **run** again.

The cat **rubbed** against Tom's leg.

skunk   See page 205

scissors   See page 195

shower   See page 201

On this page are pictures of words
that begin with the letter "S". Can
you find each word in your book?
Turn to the page number you see
near the picture. When you find the
right word you will see this: ■

sad

When you are **sad**, you feel very unhappy. Sometimes you cry when you are **sad**. Louise was **sad** because she couldn't go to the movies with us.

safe

When you are **safe**, nothing bad can happen to you. It is not **safe** to cross the street when the light is red. The dog felt **safe** under the bed during the storm.

said

Jim **said** "Do you know where my baseball glove is?"

sail

A **sail** is a large piece of cloth on a boat. When the wind blows on the **sail** it makes the boat go. We went out on the lake in a **sailboat**. David and Michael **sailed** their boats in the pond. ☼*See the picture.*

David and Michael **sailed** their boats in the pond.

salt

Salt is something that we put on food to make it taste better. **Salt** is white. The water in the ocean has **salt** in it.

same

If things are the **same**, it means that they are just alike. Bill's bicycle is the **same** as mine. All the butterflies were the **same** color. ☼*See the picture.*

All the butterflies were the **same** color.

sand

Sand is very small pieces of rock. You find **sand** on beaches and in deserts.

The toad **sat** on a rock.

sat

The toad **sat** on a rock. ☼*See the picture.*

save

1. When you **save** someone, you keep something bad from happening to them. The fireman **saved** the dog from the burning house.
2. **Save** also means that you keep something to use later. Tom **saves** his money.

saw

Lucy **saw** Tom walking along the street.

say

Say means to make words with your voice. Did I hear you **say** something?

scare

Scare means to make someone afraid. We tried to **scare** Mom by dressing up like ghosts. ☼*See the picture.*

We tried to **scare** Mom by dressing up like ghosts.

The puppy **scratched** himself with his paw.

school

School is a place where you go to learn things. I am learning to read at **school**.

science

Science is something that tells you things about the earth and everything on it. It tells about animals, plants, and other things.

scissors

Scissors are something that you use to cut things with. **Scissors** have two sharp parts that are held together in the middle. ■

scratch

Scratch means that something sharp rubs against something else. The puppy **scratched** himself with his paw. ☼*See the picture.*

screen

1. A **screen** is something you put over a window. It is made of wire. You can see through it.
2. A **screen** is also something you watch a movie or a television show on.

sea

The **sea** is salt water. The **sea** covers large parts of the earth.

second

1. **Second** means that something comes next after the first. Nancy will be the **second** person to bat. ☼*See the picture.*
2. A **second** is also a part of a minute. There are sixty **seconds** in a minute.

Nancy will be the **second** person to bat.

secret

If you know a **secret**, you know something no one else knows. The present I'm giving to my mother for her birthday is a **secret**.

see

You **see** things with your eyes. We could **see** Steve's kite high up in the sky. Have you ever **seen** an elephant?

seed

A **seed** is a part of a plant. A new plant begins to grow from a **seed**.

seem

When a thing **seems** to be something, it means that it looks like it is. Gary was so big that he **seemed** older than he really was.

seesaw

A **seesaw** is something you and someone else can play on. When you go up on one end, the other person goes down on the other end.

selfish

If you are **selfish**, it means that you only think of yourself and no one else. The children thought Pam was **selfish** when she wouldn't let them ride her new bicycle.

Linda is **selling** lemonade.

sell

If you **sell** something, it means that you give it to someone for money. Linda is **selling** lemonade. ☼*See the picture.*

send

If you **send** something, you make it go from one place to another. Mary **sent** her friend a birthday card.

The waiter **served** us ice cream for dessert.

serve

Serve means to bring food to the place where someone is going to eat it. The waiter **served** us ice cream for dessert. ☼*See the picture.*

set

1. **Set** means that you put a thing on something else. Dan **set** his books on the desk. Alice helps her mother **set** the table for dinner.
2. A **set** is also a group of things that go together. I got a new **set** of toy trains for my birthday.

sew

Sew means to hold things together with a needle and thread. Mom **sewed** the button onto my coat.

Jack made the clay into the
shape of a snake.

shadow

When the sun shines on the front of you, it
makes a **shadow** on the ground behind you.

shake

When you **shake** something, you move it up
and down very fast. **Shake** the bottle of juice
before you pour it.

shall

I **shall** be happy when I go back to school.

shape

The **shape** of something is the way it looks.
The **shape** of a ball is round. Jack made the
clay into the **shape** of a snake. ☼*See the picture.*

share

When you **share** something, you let someone
else have a part of it. Ellen **shared** her box of
cookies with us.

sharp

When a thing is **sharp**, it is easy to cut things
with it. A knife is **sharp**. An alligator has very
sharp teeth. ☼*See the picture.*

An alligator has very **sharp** teeth.

she

Mary said **she** was coming to my birthday party. **She'd** means "she had." **She'd** better clean up her room. **She'll** means "she will." **She'll** be late if she doesn't hurry. **She's** means "she is." **She's** taking her dog out for a walk.

sheep

A **sheep** is an animal. We make cloth from the hair of **sheep**.

shell

A **shell** is something hard that covers a thing. Eggs are in **shells**. My turtle has a green **shell**.

shine

Shine means to give out light. The sun **shines** in the daytime. Teddy **shined** his shoes. ☼*See the picture.* I have two **shiny** pennies.

Teddy **shined** his shoes.

ship

A **ship** is a very big boat. A **ship** can carry many people and things over the water.

shirt

A **shirt** is something to wear. It covers the top of you. Tom is wearing a red and white **shirt** that buttons in the front.

shoe

A **shoe** is something you wear on your foot.

shook

The polar bear **shook** himself dry. ☼*See the picture.*

The polar bear **shook** himself dry.

shoot

Shoot means to try to hit something with a bullet from a gun. The cowboys in the movie said they would **shoot** the bad man if he tried to run away.

shop

A **shop** is a place where you can buy things. John went to the pet **shop** to buy food for his turtle. Mom went to a **shop** to buy a new pair of shoes. We are going to **shop** for school clothes soon.

shore

The **shore** is land along the water. Dad and I fished from the **shore** of the lake.

short

When something is **short**, it means that one end of it is not far away from the other end. Harry is too **short** to reach the top shelf. Jenny has **short** hair. The dog has **short** legs. ☼*See the picture.*

The dog has **short** legs.

shot

1. A **shot** is the noise that a gun makes when it goes off.
2. A **shot** is also medicine that a doctor puts into your arm with a needle. A **shot** can keep you from getting sick.

should

George **should** help his brother clean up the playroom. Mom **should** be home soon.

shoulder

A **shoulder** is a part of your body. You have two **shoulders**. Your arms join the rest of your body at your **shoulders**.

shovel

A **shovel** is something to dig with. It has a long handle with a flat piece at one end. Matt dug a hole in the ground with his **shovel**.

show

When you **show** a thing, you let somebody see it. Mary **showed** her friends her new bicycle. ☼*See the picture.* Has Betty **shown** you the picture she drew? We saw a **show** about a dog on television last night.

Mary **showed** her friends her new bicycle.

shower

A **shower** is water coming down. Mike took a **shower** instead of a bath. ■

shut

When you **shut** something it means that you close it. Please **shut** the window so that the rain won't come in. Helen **shut** her eyes and made a wish before she blew out the candles on her birthday cake.

shy

When you are **shy** it means that you feel a little scared when there are a lot of people around. The **shy** little boy hid behind his mother when the guests came.

sick

When you are **sick**, you do not feel well. Jane had to take medicine when she was **sick**. ☼*See the picture.*

Jane had to take medicine when she was **sick**.

201

side

A **side** is one part of a thing. The **sides** of your room are the walls. Jill saw Bob riding his bicycle on the other **side** of the street. Which **side** are you playing on in the baseball game?

sidewalk

A **sidewalk** is the part of a street where cars do not go. We walk on the **sidewalk**. I like to roller-skate on the **sidewalk** in front of our house.

sight

Sight is how you see. Jimmy's **sight** got better when he started wearing glasses. The sun went out of **sight** behind a cloud.

sign

A **sign** is a thing that tells you something. I wait for the school bus near a **sign** that says "Bus Stop." The famous movie star **signed** her name for the girls. ☼*See the picture.*

The famous movie star **signed** her name for the girls.

silly

If you are **silly**, it means that you do funny things. John was **silly** when he put on two different shoes.

since

Sue got a cold last week and has been absent from school ever **since**. **Since** the car won't go, we'll have to take the bus.

sing

Sing means that you make music with your voice. The whole class will **sing** a song together. The children **sang** "Happy Birthday" to Ann. The birds in the trees began to **sing**.

There was a **single** deer in the field.

single

Single means only one. There was a **single** deer in the field. ☼*See the picture.*

sink

1. A **sink** is something that you wash things in. **Sinks** have faucets to let water into them. Wash your hands at the **sink** before dinner.
2. **Sink** also means to go down into water. Billy threw a rock into the pond and watched it **sink** to the bottom.

sister

Your **sister** is a girl who has the same mother and father as you.

sit

Sit means that you rest on the bottom part of your body. The teacher told the children to **sit** down in their chairs.

size

Size is how big or little a thing is. I wear a bigger **size** shoe than you do. Mom's clothes were the wrong **size** for Betty. ☼*See the picture.*

skate

A **skate** is something you wear on your foot. We wear ice **skates** when we **skate** on the pond.

skin

Skin is something that covers the outside of a thing. **Skin** covers your whole body. An apple has a red **skin**. An elephant has gray **skin**.

skip

Skip means that you move along by hopping first on one foot and then on the other. The children were **skipping** rope in the playground. ☼*See the picture.*

Mom's clothes were the wrong **size** for Betty.

The children were **skipping** rope in the playground.

skirt

A **skirt** is something to wear. It hangs down from your waist. Girls and women wear **skirts**. Mary wore a red sweater with her blue **skirt**.

skunk

A **skunk** is an animal. It is black with a white line down its back. Sometimes **skunks** smell very bad. ■

sky

The **sky** is what you see above you when you are outdoors. There is a moon in the **sky** at night. The sun shines in the **sky** in the daytime.

sled

A **sled** is a thing you slide over snow on. The children rode their **sleds** down the hill.

sleep

Sleep is when you rest with your eyes closed. Sometimes you dream when you **sleep**. I go to **sleep** at eight o'clock every night. Did you have a good night's **sleep**? Bobby was very **sleepy** because he stayed up late to watch television. ☼*See the picture.*

Bobby was very **sleepy** because he stayed up late to watch television.

slide

When you **slide** you move on something easily. Don is going to **slide** down the hill on his sled. A **slide** is a thing in a playground that you **slide** down.

slip

Slip means that you slide and fall down. Be careful not to **slip** on the ice. The dish **slipped** out of Ben's hand and broke on the floor.

205

A turtle walks very **slowly**.

slow

When you are **slow**, it means that you don't go very fast. Chuck was so **slow** getting dressed that he was late for school. A turtle walks very **slowly**. ☼*See the picture.*

small

When something is **small**, it means that it is not big. A mouse is a **small** animal. My younger sister is **smaller** than I am.

smell

Smell means that you know something by using your nose. Tim could **smell** cookies baking when he went into the kitchen.

smile

When you **smile** you turn up the corners of your mouth. A **smile** shows that you are happy. The man told everyone to **smile** when he took the picture. ☼*See the picture.*

GRADE 2E
NORWOOD
SCHOOL

The man told everyone to **smile** when he took the **picture.**

smoke

Smoke is something that comes from a thing that is burning. **Smoke** came from the building that was on fire.

smooth

If something is **smooth** it means that it doesn't feel rough when you touch it. The top of my desk is **smooth**.

snake

A **snake** is a long, thin animal. **Snakes** don't have legs. **Snakes** move by sliding along on the ground.

snap

Snap means to make a quick noise. When Hank **snaps** his fingers his dog always comes.

sneeze

When you **sneeze**, you blow air out of your mouth and nose in a loud way. I always **sneeze** a lot when I have a cold.

snow

Snow is rain that freezes in the sky. **Snow** comes down in little white pieces called **snowflakes**. When it **snows** the children get out their sleds. Linda and Jim are making a **snowman.**

It was **so** cold that the lake was frozen.

so

It was **so** cold that the lake was frozen. ☼*See the picture.*

My kitten has **soft** fur.

soap

Soap is something you wash and clean with. Lou washed his hands with **soap** and water.

sock

A **sock** is something you wear on your foot. You wear **socks** inside your shoes.

soda

A **soda** is something to drink. It has little bubbles in it and it tastes sweet.

soft

Soft means that something is not hard. My kitten has **soft** fur. ☼*See the picture.*

sold

Dad **sold** our old car and bought a new one.

soldier

A **soldier** is someone who is in an army.

some

Jeff would like **some** ice cream. **Some** of the birds were eating the bread we gave them. ☼*See the picture.*

somebody

There is **somebody** at the front door. **Someone** let the dog out.

somersault

Somersault means that you roll your body so your feet go over your head.

something

Linda saw **something** on the sidewalk and picked it up. **Something** is wrong with our TV set.

Some of the birds were eating the bread we gave them.

sometimes

Sometimes we go to the beach in the summer. Mom **sometimes** lets me stay up late to watch TV.

son

A **son** is a child who is a boy or a man. Christopher is the **son** of his mother and father.

song

A **song** is something that you sing. A **song** has words and music. The children sang the **songs** that the teacher taught them. ☼*See the picture.*

The children sang the **songs** that the teacher taught them.

soon

If something is going to happen **soon** it means that it will happen in a very short time. School will start **soon**.

sore

If you feel **sore** it means that something hurts you. Betty has a **sore** finger.

sorry

If you are **sorry** about something it means that you are sad about it. Debbie was **sorry** that she broke the dish. ☼*See the picture.*

sound

A **sound** is something that you hear. Thunder makes a loud **sound**.

soup

Soup is something to eat. **Soup** is made with water or milk. I like tomato **soup** for lunch.

Debbie was **sorry** that she broke the dish.

sour

When something is **sour** it means that it does not taste sweet. A lemon has a **sour** taste. ☀*See the picture.*

south

When you look at a map, the bottom part is **south**. If you face the sun when it goes down in the evening, **south** is on your left.

space

Space is a place between things. Mom found a **space** to park the car in. The moon and the planets are in **space**.

spank

Spank means to hit something with your hand open. Mom **spanked** Mary for kicking her brother.

speak

Speak means that you say words. I'm going to **speak** to my grandmother over the telephone.

special

When something is **special**, it is not like anything else. Your birthday is a **special** day to you.

spell

Spell means that you use letters in a special way to make a word. Can you **spell** your name?

spend

Spend means that you pay money for something. Jerry is going to **spend** fifty cents for a comic book. Helen **spent** ten cents for a lollipop.

A lemon has a **sour** taste.

spider

A **spider** is a kind of bug. It has eight legs and no wings.

spill

When you **spill** something, you let it fall out of a thing. The baby **spilled** her milk. ☼*See the picture.*

spin

When you **spin,** it means that you go around and around. Dan tried to **spin** around on the ice.

splash

When you **splash** it means that you throw water around. The seal **splashed** into the water. ☼*See the picture.* Joan jumped into the pool with a big **splash**.

The baby **spilled** her milk.

The seal **splashed** into the water.

spoon

A **spoon** is a thing that you use for eating food with. It has a handle and a round part at one end. We eat ice cream and pudding with a **spoon**.

A leopard has **spots** on its body.

spot

A **spot** is a small mark on something. Jack has **spots** of mud on his shoes. A leopard has **spots** on its body. ☼*See the picture.*

spring

Spring is a time of the year. **Spring** comes between winter and summer.

square

A **square** is something that has four sides. The sides of a **square** are the same size. The candy came in a **square** box. ☼*See the picture.*

squeeze

Squeeze means that you push hard on something. Tom **squeezed** toothpaste onto his toothbrush. Mother **squeezes** juice from oranges.

squirrel

A **squirrel** is a small animal. **Squirrels** have big tails and live in trees.

stairs

Stairs are a set of steps for going up or down in a house. The children went up the **stairs** to their rooms.

The candy came in a **square** box.

The bus was full, so Dad had to **stand**.

stand

When you **stand** it means that you are on your feet. The bus was full, so Dad had to **stand**. ☼*See the picture.*

star

A **star** is a small, bright light that you can see in the sky at night. **Stars** are very, very far away from us.

stare

When you **stare** at something, it means that you look at it a long time. Jennifer **stared** at the cakes and cookies in the bakery window.

start

Start means that you begin to do something. What time do you **start** off for school? The movie **starts** in ten minutes. Dad **started** the engine of the boat.

state

A **state** is one part of your country. Ann lives in the **state** of Texas. There are fifty **states** in the United States of America.

station

A **station** is a place where something special is done. A gas **station** is a place where we get gas for a car. We get on a train at a train **station**. Policemen work in police **stations**. A radio program comes from a radio **station**.

stay

Stay means that you don't move from a place. Kenny had to **stay** in bed because he had a bad cold. ☼*See the picture.* We **stayed** at school for lunch.

steal

Steal means to take something that doesn't belong to you. The man tried to **steal** money from the bank, but the police caught him.

step

A **step** is a place where you put your foot when you walk. Someone is coming up the front **steps** of our house. Be careful not to **step** in that mud puddle.

stick

1. A **stick** is a long piece of wood. Joe threw a **stick** for his dog to run and get. Alice ate a **stick** of candy.
2. **Stick** also means to push something into something else. Bob is trying to **stick** a pin into Helen's balloon.

still

1. If you are **still**, it means that you are not moving or making any noise. Mom told us to keep **still** while she was talking on the phone. The little boy wouldn't sit **still**.
2. If something is **still** happening, it means that it is happening now. It is **still** raining out.

Kenny had to **stay** in bed because he had a bad cold.

214

stir

Stir means to move something around and around with a thing. Mom **stirred** the paint before she painted the chair. ☼*See the picture.*

stomach

Your **stomach** is a part of your body. Food goes into your **stomach** after you swallow it.

stone

A **stone** is a piece of rock. Buildings are made of **stone**.

stood

Joe **stood** up when the teacher came in.

stop

Stop means to not do something any more. The train **stopped** so that the people could get off. ☼*See the picture.*

Mom **stirred** the paint before she painted the chair.

The train **stopped** so that the people could get off.

store

A **store** is a place where you buy things. Mom buys food at the grocery **store**. Dad took us to the shoe **store** to buy us new shoes.

storm

A **storm** is a time when it rains or snows a lot. Sometimes there is thunder and lightning during a **storm**.

story

A **story** is something that you tell someone. Grandpa told us some **stories** about fairies.

stove

A **stove** is a thing to cook on. We have **stoves** in our kitchens.

straight

Straight means that something is flat. Dad wanted to make sure the picture was hanging **straight** on the wall. ☼*See the picture.* Sit up **straight** at your desk.

strange

When something is **strange**, it means that it seems very different to you. Tom's new school is still **strange** to him. Bruce drew a **strange** looking animal with pink ears and a red tail.

straw

A **straw** is a thing that you drink something through. Gary is drinking his soda through a **straw**.

strawberry

A **strawberry** is something to eat. It is a small, red fruit.

Dad wanted to make sure the picture was hanging **straight** on the wall.

street

A **street** is a road in a town or city. What **street** do you live on? Our **street** has a lot of houses on it.

stretch

Stretch means to make something longer. The giraffe **stretched** its neck to reach the leaves. ☼*See the picture.*

strike

Strike means that you hit something. You try to **strike** the ball with a bat in baseball.

string

String is a thin line of something. Dad used **string** to tie up the box. Tommy flew his kite on a **string**.

strong

If you are **strong**, it means that you can lift heavy things. Jerry was not **strong** enough to move the heavy desk. The wind was so **strong** that it blew down a big tree. An elephant is a **strong** animal. ☼*See the picture.*

The giraffe **stretched** its neck to reach the leaves.

217

An elephant is a **strong** animal.

Our car got **stuck** in the mud.

stuck

Lucy **stuck** a pin in the balloon. Our car got **stuck** in the mud. ☼*See the picture.*

student

A **student** is someone who is learning things at school. There are lots of **students** at my school.

stuff

Stuff is lots of things. I have some **stuff** in my closet that I don't play with any more. The **stuff** in the pillow is feathers.

stung

A bee **stung** Judy on her arm.

stupid

If people do something **stupid** it means that they are not thinking very much about what they are doing.

subtract

Subtract means to make a number less. If you **subtract** 3 from 7, you get 4.

such

I have never seen **such** a pretty doll. We had **such** a nice time at the party!

sudden

When something is **sudden**, it means that it happens very quickly. **Suddenly**, it began to rain. ☼*See the picture.*

sugar

Sugar is something that you put in food to make it sweet. I put **sugar** on my cereal. There is **sugar** in candy.

suit

A **suit** is something to wear. A **suit** is a jacket with a pair of pants or with a skirt.

suitcase

A **suitcase** is something you carry clothes in. A **suitcase** is flat and has a handle. You pack a **suitcase** when you are going on a trip.

summer

Summer is a time of the year. **Summer** comes between spring and fall.

sun

The **sun** is the thing that shines in the sky in the daytime. The **sun** makes you warm.

Suddenly, it began to rain.

suppose

1. Suppose means that you think something might be true. I **suppose** that I will have a party on my birthday.

2. If you are **supposed** to do something, it means that you should do it. I'm **supposed** to go home right after school.

sure

If you are **sure** about something, it means that you know that it is true. Mary is **sure** that she gave the right answer. I'm **sure** that I'm going to visit my friend tomorrow.

surprise

A **surprise** is something that you don't know about ahead of time. The birthday present Rick got was a real **surprise** to him. Dad **surprised** Mom by bringing her flowers as a present. ☼*See the picture.*

Dad **surprised** Mom by bringing her flowers as a present.

swallow

When you **swallow** food, you make it go down your throat to your stomach. John was so thirsty that he **swallowed** the water quickly.

swamp

A **swamp** is land that is very wet.

sweater

A **sweater** is something to wear. It covers the top of you. You pull a **sweater** on over your head or button it up the front.

sweep

Sweep means that you clean something with a broom. Tom is **sweeping** the kitchen floor. ☼*See the picture.*

Tom is **sweeping** the kitchen floor.

sweet

If something tastes **sweet**, it means that it has a nice taste like sugar. Ice cream is **sweet**.

swell

Swell means that something grows bigger. If you blow air into a balloon, it will **swell**.

swim

Swim means to move in the water by using your arms and legs. We will **swim** in the lake this summer. Mark **swam** across the pool. Shirley is the best **swimmer** in our class.

swing

A **swing** is a thing that you can sit on and move up and down in the air. We have a **swing** in our yard that hangs from a tree. Tom likes to **swing** in the playground. Uncle Eddie **swung** me in the air. ☼*See the picture.*

Uncle Eddie **swung** me in the air.

221

truck   See page 236

telephone   See page 225

T t

turtle   See page 237

On this page are pictures of words that begin with the letter "T". Can you find each word in your book? Turn to the page number you see near the picture. When you find the right word you will see this: ■

tiger   See page 231

table

A **table** is a thing to put things on. It has a flat top and four legs. We helped Mom put the food on the **table**.

tag

Tag is a game in which someone called "it," chases everyone else until he or she touches someone. The person who is touched then becomes "it" and he or she has to chase the others.

tail

A **tail** is a part of an animal's body. It sticks out from the back end. Cats and dogs have **tails**.

take

Mom reached down to **take** my hand as we crossed the street. Dad is going to **take** us to the movies this afternoon. ☼*See the picture.* My sister **takes** a bus to work. We are **taking** some sandwiches and lemonade on our picnic. Let's **take** a walk through the park. Are you going to **take** my picture? If you **take** 3 from 4, you have 1. It has **taken** us a long time to walk to your house.

talk

Talk means to say words. The baby cannot **talk** yet. I **talked** to him last week. My cousin and I had a nice long **talk** on the telephone.

tall

If something is **tall**, it means that it goes up far from the ground. That is a **tall** building. A giraffe is a **tall** animal. ☼*See the picture.* Dad is six feet **tall**.

Dad is going to **take** us to the movies this afternoon.

A giraffe is a **tall** animal.

223

Mom let us **taste** the pudding she was making for dessert.

taste

Taste is the way food feels when you put it in your mouth. I like the **taste** of chocolate cake. Mom let us **taste** the pudding she was making for dessert. ☼*See the picture.* The cookie **tasted** very sweet.

taxi

A **taxi** is a car. You pay the driver of a **taxi** to take you someplace. A **taxi** is the same thing as a **cab**. We took a **taxi** to the airport.

tea

Tea is something to drink. Mom drinks **tea** at breakfast.

teach

Teach means to help someone learn how to do something. Mrs. Smith **taught** us how to write our names in school today. My sister is **teaching** me how to ride a bicycle. ☼*See the picture.* Mr. Edwards is our **teacher**.

team

A **team** is a group of people that plays a game together. I want to be on the football **team** when I get older. Baseball is a game that is played with two **teams**.

My sister is **teaching** me how to ride a bicycle.

224

tear

1. Tear means to pull something apart. This word sounds like **hair**. Jerry **tore** his shirt on the fence. ☼*See the picture.*

2. A **tear** is also a drop of water that comes out of your eyes when you cry. This word sounds like **here**. Mom wiped the **tears** from the baby's eyes.

tease

Tease means to make fun of someone. The players on the other team all **teased** Jeff when he missed the ball.

teenager

A **teenager** is someone who is between the ages of thirteen and nineteen. My brother is a **teenager**.

teeth

Teeth is more than one tooth. Larry has lost his two front **teeth**.

telephone

A **telephone** is a thing that you use when you talk to someone who is far away from you. A **telephone** has wires that carry the sound of your voice. A **telephone** is the same thing as a **phone**. ■

television

A **television** is a thing that you can turn on to look at and listen to. You watch different programs on **television**.

tell

Tell means to say something. Did you **tell** your friends about your new kitten? Mom **tells** us stories before we go to sleep.

Jerry **tore** his shirt on the fence.

temperature

Temperature is a word that tells how hot or cold something is. The **temperature** outside is very cold in the winter.

tennis

Tennis is a game. It is played by two people who hit a ball to each other.

test

A **test** is something that shows how much you know about something. A **test** has problems for you to do or questions that you have to answer.

The mother cat is bigger **than** her kittens.

than

The mother cat is bigger **than** her kittens. ☼*See the picture.* I would rather play outside **than** watch television.

thank

Thank means to say that you are happy about what someone gave you or did for you. Bob **thanked** his brother for the birthday present. Mary said **"Thanks"** to Tom for fixing her bicycle.

Thanksgiving

Thanksgiving is a day when we remember and give thanks for all the good things we have. It comes at the end of November.

that

That girl is my sister. This is a toy plane and **that** is a real one. ☼*See the picture.* I'm sorry **that** you are sick.

This is a toy plane and **that** is a real one.

the

Please close **the** door. **The** sun is bright.

226

their

Their house is the one at the end of the street. These books are ours and those are **theirs**.

them

I saw **them** at the store. My friends asked me if I wanted to play ball with **them**.

then

The game ended and **then** we went home. If you don't want your cake, **then** give it to me. I hope to have my homework finished before **then**.

there

There is no more pie. Mom said, "Put the box over **there**." ☼*See the picture.* We walked to the park, and we saw Jane **there**.

thermometer

A **thermometer** is a thing that you use to find out how hot or cold something is. The **thermometer** showed that it was cold outside.

Mom said, "Put the box over **there**."

these

These gloves are mine and those are yours. **These** are very pretty flowers.

they

Susan and Jack were late for school because **they** missed the bus. **They'd** means "they had." **They'd** better do all their homework. **They'll** means "they will." **They'll** go to the beach tomorrow. **They're** means "they are." **They're** going to the circus today.

A bear has **thick** fur.

thick

When something is **thick**, it is big around.
Dad cut the **thick** piece of wood with a saw.
A bear has **thick** fur. ☼*See the picture.*

thin

When something is **thin**, it is not very big
around. A baby horse has **thin** legs. ☼*See the
picture.* Mom cut me a **thin** piece of cake.

thing

A book is a **thing**. Please pick up the **things**
on the floor. Helping your mother carry the
packages was a nice **thing** to do.

think

Think means to use your mind. The teacher
told us to **think** very hard before we
answered the questions on the test. Jack
thinks Marion will win the race.

third

When something is **third**, it is next after the
second thing. My sister is in the **third** grade.

A baby horse has **thin** legs.

thirsty

When you are **thirsty**, you want something to drink. We were so **thirsty** that we drank lots and lots of lemonade.

this

This coat is mine. **This** is his and that is hers.

those

These toy cars are mine and **those** are my brother's. ☼*See the picture.*

though

I was late for school, **though** I got up early.

thought

I **thought** Dad was going to take us to the zoo.

thread

Thread is very, very thin string that is used for sewing.

threw

Ted and Judy **threw** snowballs at each other. ☼*See the picture.*

These toy cars are mine and **those** are my brother's.

229

Ted and Judy **threw** snowballs at each other.

Rick hammered the nail **through** the piece of wood.

My little sister is learning how to **tie** her shoes.

throat

The **throat** is a part of your body. It goes from your mouth to your stomach. When I was sick my **throat** was sore.

through

Rick hammered the nail **through** the piece of wood. ☼*See the picture.* Are you **through** with your homework yet?

throw

Throw means to send something through the air. Jim and Andy like to **throw** the ball to each other. Dad has **thrown** away all the old newspapers.

thumb

The **thumb** is the short, thick finger on your hand. Your **thumb** makes it easier to pick things up with your hand.

thunder

Thunder is a loud sound in the sky that comes after lightning. **Thunder** comes during a storm.

ticket

A **ticket** is a piece of paper that shows you have paid to do something. You need a **ticket** to ride on a train or an airplane. We gave our **tickets** to the man at the door when we went to the movie.

tie

When you **tie** something, you hold it together by putting a string or ribbon around it. My little sister is learning how to **tie** her shoes. ☼*See the picture.* Mike **tied** the present with a red ribbon.

tiger

A **tiger** is a big animal. It has yellow fur with black lines on it. ■

Tony kept a **tight** hold on the dog's leash so that it wouldn't run away.

tight

When you hold something **tight**, you hold it so that you won't drop it. Mother held my hand **tight** when we crossed the street. Tony kept a **tight** hold on the dog's leash so that it wouldn't run away. ☼*See the picture.*

time

Time is when something happens. What **time** is it? It is **time** for lunch. We had a good **time** at the beach today.

tiny

If something is **tiny**, it is very small. An ant is a **tiny** insect.

tired

When you are **tired**, you do not feel like doing very much. Dad was **tired** after he cut down the tree. ☼*See the picture.*

Dad was **tired** after he cut down the tree.

to

I am going **to** school. Joan gave the candy **to** her brother. Gary is learning **to** swim.

toast

Toast is bread that has been made brown by cooking. We eat **toast** with butter on it for breakfast.

today

Today is the day that it is now. **Today** is my birthday. Do you want to go ice skating **today**?

toe

A **toe** is a part of your foot. You have five **toes** at the end of each foot.

together

Mom mixed the sugar and butter **together**. The animals stood **together** in the field. ☼*See the picture.*

The animals stood **together** in the field.

told

Grandpa **told** us stories about the things he did when he was a little boy. ☼*See the picture.*

tomato

A **tomato** is something to eat. It is round and full of juice. **Tomatoes** are red.

tomorrow

Tomorrow is the day after today. If today is Saturday, then **tomorrow** is Sunday.

tongue

The **tongue** is a part of your mouth. You use your **tongue** when you speak.

tonight

Tonight is the night of the day that it is now.

too

Sara felt sick because she ate **too** much candy. George and Jimmy like to play basketball, and their little brother does **too**.

took

Jim **took** his books to school.

tooth

A **tooth** is one of the hard, white parts in your mouth. Your **teeth** are used for biting and chewing food.

top

The **top** of something is the highest part. Gloria climbed to the **top** of the jungle gym. ☼*See the picture.* Please put the **top** on the box.

Grandpa **told** us stories about the things he did when he was a little boy.

Gloria climbed to the **top** of the jungle gym.

233

The puppies ran **toward** their mother.

touch

Touch means to put your hand on something. Bill **touched** the hot iron and burned his finger.

toward

The puppies ran **toward** their mother. ☼*See the picture.* We walked **towards** the park.

towel

A **towel** is a thing you use to dry something with. I use a **towel** after my bath. You dry dishes with a **towel**.

tower

A **tower** is a tall part on a building. The church had a high **tower** with bells in it.

town

A **town** is a place where people live and work. A **town** has houses and other buildings in it. It is smaller than a city.

toy

A **toy** is a thing to play with. A doll, a kite, and a ball are **toys**. I let my baby sister play with my **toys**.

track

A **track** is one of the long metal pieces that the wheels of a train go on. It is dangerous to walk on the railroad **tracks**.

trade

Trade means to give a person something of yours for something of theirs. Mike **traded** one of his toy cars for one of Ronnie's. ☼*See the picture.* David asked me to **trade** seats with him so he could sit next to Betsy.

Mike **traded** one of his toy cars for one of Ronnie's.

traffic

Traffic is cars and trucks moving along the same road. There is not much **traffic** on the street where I live.

train

A **train** is a line of railroad cars that are joined together. It is pulled by an engine that makes it go. We took the **train** when we went to visit my grandmother.

travel

Travel means to go from one place to another. We **traveled** by car on our vacation.

tree

A **tree** is a tall plant that has a trunk. **Trees** also have branches and leaves.

trick

A **trick** is something you do when you are trying to make people think you are doing something else. Jack slammed the door as a **trick** to make everyone think he had left. Jane is teaching her dog a **trick**. ☼*See the picture.* Beth tried to **trick** me into thinking she was asleep.

tricycle

A **tricycle** is something to ride on. It has two wheels in the back and one in front.

trip

1. **Trip** means to hit your foot on something and almost fall. Mark **tripped** on the fallen branch. ☼*See the picture.*
2. A **trip** is also when you go from one place to another. We took a car **trip** to visit my grandmother.

Jane is teaching her dog a **trick**.

Mark **tripped** on the fallen branch.

235

trouble

1. When someone is in **trouble**, it means that they have done something wrong and that people are mad at them. Clara knew she was going to be in **trouble** when her mother found out she had broken the lamp.

2. Trouble also means something hard to do. Jack had **trouble** moving the heavy box.

truck

A **truck** is something to ride in. It has wheels and a motor to make it go. **Trucks** carry big things from one place to another. When we moved, they put all our furniture in a **truck** to take it to our new house. ■

true

When something is **true**, it means that it is not a lie. Is it **true** that Ted will be going to our school next year?

trunk

1. A **trunk** is the main part of a tree. It has bark on it. The branches grow out from the **trunk**.

2. A **trunk** is also the long nose of an elephant. The elephant uses his **trunk** to pick things up.

truth

If something you say is true, then you are telling the **truth**. Jenny told the **truth** when her father asked her if she had broken her brother's truck.

try

When you **try** to do something, you find out if you can do it. Billy **tried** to lift the log, but it was too heavy. ☼*See the picture.*

Billy **tried** to lift the log, but it was too heavy.

Dad **turned** to look behind him before he backed the car up.

turn

1. Turn means to move around. The **wheels**
of a bicycle **turn**. **Turn** the paper over and
write your name on it. Dad **turned** to look
behind him before he backed the car up.
☼*See the picture.*
2. A **turn** is also a chance to do something.
It's Johnny's **turn** to bat.

turtle

A **turtle** is an animal. It has a hard shell on
the outside of its body and very short legs.
Turtles live on land and in the water. ∎

TV

A **TV** is a thing that you can turn on to look
at and listen to. You watch different programs
on **TV**. A **TV** is the same as a **television**.

twice

If you do something **twice**, you do it two
times. I read that book **twice**.

umbrella   See page 239

Uu Vv

vegetable   See page 240

On this page are pictures of words that begin with the letters "U" and "V". Can you find each word in your book? Turn to the page number you see near the picture. When you find the right word you will see this: ■

umbrella

An **umbrella** is a thing that you hold over your head to keep the rain off. ■

uncle

Your **uncle** is your father or mother's brother. Your aunt's husband is also your **uncle**.

under

We sat **under** an umbrella at the beach because it was so hot. ☼*See the picture.* Beth is wearing a blue dress **under** her coat.

understand

When you **understand** something, it means that you know something. Steve **understood** the teacher's question. I don't **understand** why my sister is mad at me.

undress

Undress means to take off your clothes. My little sister can **undress** herself.

unhappy

When you are **unhappy**, you are sad. Ellen was **unhappy** because her favorite record was broken. ☼*See the picture.*

United States

The **United States** is a country. It is also called the **United States of America**.

unless

You can't borrow my bicycle **unless** you promise to give it back. The game will be played tomorrow **unless** it rains.

We sat **under** an umbrella at the beach because it was so hot.

Ellen was **unhappy** because her favorite record was broken.

The cat is **up** in the tree.

Mom **used** a shovel to dig a hole for the plant.

until

Dad said he would wait **until** I got in bed before he told me the story. We go to school from nine o'clock **until** three.

up

The cat is **up** in the tree. ☼*See the picture.* We looked **up** to see the airplane. Jane turned **up** the sound on the television. My brother didn't get **up** till nine o'clock this morning.

upstairs

If you go **upstairs**, you go up the stairs to another floor.

us

Dad took **us** to the circus. Our teacher gave **us** a party at the end of the school year.

use

Use means to do something with something else. You **use** your nose to smell. Mom **used** a shovel to dig a hole for the plant. ☼*See the picture.* Jim is **using** my book to do his homework.

usually

Usually means very often. It is **usually** hot in the summer.

vacation

A **vacation** is a time when people do not work or go to school. Our school's summer **vacation** starts tomorrow. We are going to the beach when my father has his **vacation.**

vegetable

A **vegetable** is a plant. Carrots, potatoes, and lettuce are **vegetables.** ■

A rhinoceros is a **very** big animal.

very

I can run **very** fast. A rhinoceros is a **very** big animal. ☼*See the picture.*

visit

Visit means to go see someone. Uncle Dennis came to **visit** us. ☼*See the picture.* A **visitor** is someone who **visits**. My mother is having **visitors** this afternoon.

voice

The **voice** is the sound you make through your mouth. You speak or sing with your **voice**.

vote

Vote means to say if you are for or against something. We are going to **vote** for the class president by raising our hands.

Uncle Dennis came to **visit** us.

241

wagon   See page 243

Ww

witch   See page 250

On this page are pictures of words that begin with the letter "W". Can you find each word in your book? Turn to the page number you see near the picture. When you find the right word you will see this: ■

wolf   See page 251

wagon

A **wagon** is something to ride in or carry things in. It has four wheels. Bobby pulled his sister in his **wagon.** ■

wait

Wait means to stay in a place. When you **wait**, you stay until someone comes or something happens. Dad and I were **waiting** for Mom to sit down so we could eat. ☼*See the picture.* We **waited** on the corner for the school bus.

wake

Wake means to stop sleeping. What time do you **wake** up in the morning? If you are not quiet, you will **wake** the baby.

walk

Walk means to go by moving your feet. My older brother **walks** to school. We took a **walk** through the park.

wall

A **wall** is one side of a room. Mom hung the pictures I drew on the **walls** in my room.

want

When you **want** something, it means that you would like to have it. Nancy **wants** a kite for her birthday. The dog **wanted** its dinner. ☼*See the picture.*

war

A **war** is a fight between countries. An army fights in a **war.**

Dad and I were **waiting** for Mom to sit down so we could eat.

The dog **wanted** its dinner.

warm

When something is **warm**, it means that it is more hot than cold. The blanket kept me **warm**.

was

Who **was** at the door? **Wasn't** means "was not." Jim **wasn't** in school today.

We helped Dad **wash** the car.

wash

Wash means to clean something by putting water and soap on it. Mom told us to **wash** our hands before dinner. We helped Dad **wash** the car. ☼*See the picture.*

watch

1. **Watch** means to look at something. Mom let me **watch** television all afternoon when I was sick. The lifeguard **watched** the children while they swam in the pool.

2. A **watch** is also a thing to wear that shows you what time it is.

water

Water is the liquid that is in the oceans, lakes, rivers, and ponds. We drink **water.**

way

1. The **way** you do something is how you do it. Being nice to other people is a good **way** to make friends.
2. **Way** also means a road that goes from one place to another. We pass Tim's house on our **way** to school.

we

We are going to school. **We'd** means "we had." **We'd** just gone outside when it began to rain. **We'll** means "we will." **We'll** go to the park this afternoon. **We're** means "we are." **We're** going to the zoo. **We've** means "we have." **We've** seen that movie twice.

wear

Wear means to have something on your body. Mom said, "**Wear** your raincoat or else you'll get wet." ☼*See the picture.*

weather

Weather is what it is like outdoors. I wear my warm coat when the **weather** is cold.

week

A **week** is seven days. The days of the **week** are Sunday, Monday, Tuesday, Wednesday, Thursday, Friday, Saturday.

Mom said, "**Wear** your raincoat or else you'll get wet."

The man at the store **weighed** the tomatoes we bought.

weigh

When you **weigh** something, you find out how heavy it is. The man at the store **weighed** the tomatoes we bought. ☼*See the picture.* I **weigh** sixty pounds.

weight

Weight is how heavy something is. My **weight** is sixty pounds.

well

When you do something **well**, you do it in a good way. Robin plays the piano **well**. Terry went home from school because she didn't feel **well**.

went

My sister and I **went** to the beach today.

were

We **were** having such a good time at the playground that we didn't want to go home. **Weren't** means "were not." We **weren't** late for school even though we missed the bus.

west

The **west** is the place where the sun goes down in the evening.

wet

When something is **wet**, it has water in it. We hung the **wet** clothes out to dry. The wall Dad painted is still **wet**. ☼*See the picture.*

whale

A **whale** is a very large animal. It looks something like a fish. **Whales** live in the ocean.

what

What are you eating? **What** did you say?

wheel

A **wheel** is something round. **Wheels** help cars and bicycles move. My toy truck has four **wheels**. Roller skates have **wheels**.

when

When do you leave for school? **When** does that TV program start?

where

Where do you live? The dog showed us **where** Tommy was hiding. ☼*See the picture.*

which

Which of the books did you like best? **Which** dog is yours?

while

Let's stop playing and rest for a **while**. Our neighbor took care of our dog **while** we were on vacation.

The wall Dad painted is still **wet**.

The dog showed us **where** Tommy was hiding.

Jean **whispered** a secret to her friend Mary.

whisper

Whisper means to say something in a very soft voice. Jean **whispered** a secret to her friend Mary. ☼*See the picture.*

who

Who took my pencil? Do you know **who** left this book here?

whole

When something is **whole**, it does not have anything missing from it. Bruce ate the **whole** bar of candy by himself. Cleaning the yard was an easy job because the **whole** family helped. ☼*See the picture.*

Cleaning the yard was an easy job because the **whole** family helped.

whose

Whose coat is this? **Whose** roller skates are those?

why

Do you know **why** Carolyn can't come to the picnic with us? **Why** are you laughing?

wide

If something is **wide**, it is very big from one side to the other. The new road is **wide**. The chair was too **wide** to fit through the door. ☼*See the picture.*

wife

A **wife** is a woman who is married. Your mother is your father's **wife**.

wild

A **wild** animal is an animal that does not usually live with people. We see tigers, zebras, monkeys, and other **wild** animals at the zoo.

will

Will you help me with my homework? We **will** go to the park tomorrow.

The chair was too **wide** to fit through the door.

win

Win means to do something better than any other person who is trying to do the same thing. I think Dave will **win** the race, because he can run faster than anyone else.

wind

The **wind** is the air that moves over the earth. The **wind** blew the leaves on the ground all over the front yard. We like to fly our kites on **windy** days.

249

window

A **window** is an open place in a wall. **Windows** let in air and light. **Windows** have glass in them. Please close the **window** so the cold air won't come in.

wing

A **wing** is a thing that is used for flying. Birds and insects have **wings**. Airplanes have **wings** too.

winter

Winter is a time of the year. **Winter** comes between fall and spring.

wipe

Wipe means to clean a thing by rubbing it on something else. Please **wipe** your shoes on the rug outside the door before you come into the house. Dad **wiped** up the juice the baby had spilled. ☼*See the picture.*

wire

A **wire** is a thin piece of metal. **Wire** can be used to make fences and cages. **Wire** can also be used to carry electricity or the sounds of people's voices. Telephones have **wires**.

wish

Wish means to want something very much. Ruth **wished** that she would win the race. Billy's one **wish** is to be a policeman when he grows up.

witch

A **witch** is a person who is supposed to do magic things. Most people think **witches** are make-believe. My sister Judy dressed as a **witch** for Halloween. ■

Dad **wiped** up the juice the baby had spilled.

with

Joe and Pete went to the baseball game **with** their father. ☼*See the picture.* The boy **with** the red jacket on is my brother. Tim dug a hole **with** a shovel.

without

Helen was in such a hurry, she left **without** saying good-by to us.

woke

I **woke** up when my mother called me to get out of bed.

wolf

A **wolf** is an animal. It looks like a dog. **Wolves** usually live where it is cold. ■

woman

A **woman** is a grown-up female person. My mother and grandmother are **women**.

won

Susie **won** the swimming race. ☼*See the picture.*

Joe and Pete went to the baseball game **with** their father.

Susie **won** the swimming race.

won't

Won't means "will not." Carl **won't** be able to play with us today, because he's sick.

wood

Wood is what trees are made of. People use **wood** to build houses.

word

A **word** is a thing that we use when we talk or write. "Book" and "go" are **words**.

wore

Marie **wore** a red ribbon in her hair.

work

Work is what someone does to make money to live on. What kind of **work** do your mother and father do? My mother **works** in a library. The girls **worked** hard raking up the leaves. ☼*See the picture.*

The girls **worked** hard raking up the leaves.

world

The **world** is where all people live. The **world** is the same thing as the **earth**.

worm

A **worm** is an animal. It is long and has no legs. **Worms** move by crawling on the ground.

worry

When you **worry** it means that you feel unhappy about something. Mom starts to **worry** if we are late coming home from school.

would

Last summer we **would** go to the beach every day. **Wouldn't** means "would not." **Wouldn't** you like some more ice cream?

wrist

Your **wrist** is a part of your body. It is between your arm and your hand. You can bend your **wrist**.

write

Write means to put words on something. You can write with a pencil, a pen, or a crayon. You **write** on a piece of paper or a blackboard. Nancy has **written** her name in her book. Mark is **writing** a letter to his grandfather. Nancy **wrote** the day of her birthday on the calendar. ☼*See the picture.*

wrong

When something is **wrong** it means that it is not right. Ted's answer to the question was **wrong**. It is **wrong** to lie to people. Mary looked silly when she put the **wrong** shoes on. ☼*See the picture.*

Nancy **wrote** the day of her birthday on the calendar.

Mary looked silly when she put the **wrong** shoes on.

yard   See page 255

Xx Yy Zz

xylophone   See page 255

On this page are pictures of words that begin with the letters "X", "Y", and "Z". Can you find each word in your book? Turn to the page number you see near the picture. When you find the right word you will see this: ■

zebra   See page 256

X ray

An X **ray** is a kind of picture. The doctor took an X **ray** of Tom's arm to see if the bone was broken.

xylophone

A **xylophone** is a thing that makes music. It has a row of pieces of wood. You play a **xylophone** by hitting the pieces of wood with a kind of hammer.

yard

A **yard** is a piece of land around a house. My dog likes to run in the **yard**. We have a swing in our **yard**.

yawn

Yawn means to open your mouth wide and take a deep breath. You **yawn** when you are sleepy.

year

A **year** is twelve months. He is four **years** old.

yell

Yell means to say something in a very loud voice. Betty **yells** when she's angry. Gene gave a **yell** when he saw his new drum.

yes

Yes, you may stay up late tonight and watch television.

yesterday

Yesterday is the day before today. If today is Monday, then **yesterday** was Sunday.

yet

Sue is not old enough **yet** to go to school.

you

Are **you** coming to play with me today? **You'd** means "you had." **You'd** better hurry. **You'll** means "you will." **You'll** have fun at the party. **You're** means "you are." **You're** not as tall as I am. **You've** means "you have." **You've** spilled your milk.

young

When you are **young**, it means that you have not lived for very long. You are **young** when you are two years old.

your

Let's play at **your** house. Is this book **yours**? Be careful not to burn **yourself** on that hot iron.

zebra

A **zebra** is an animal. **Zebras** are white with black stripes. A **zebra** looks like a horse.

zero

Zero means nothing. If you have **zero** pennies, it means that you don't have any pennies at all.

zipper

A **zipper** is a thing that holds something together. **Zippers** are used on clothes. Does your jacket close with a **zipper** or with buttons?

zoo

A **zoo** is a place where you can look at animals. The animals in **zoos** are kept in cages. We saw the monkeys and the elephants at the **zoo**.

Our Wonderful World

This picture shows you what our earth looks like from outer space. Underneath the swirling white clouds you can see the blue oceans and the brown land. Did you know that most of the earth is covered with water? That is why so much of it looks blue from outer space.

This section of your book will tell you all about our world.

Our Earth

Our earth is a huge ball, far bigger than we can imagine.
It is one of nine huge balls that move around the sun.
These balls are called *planets*.

The earth moves around the sun once a year. The path
the earth travels is called an *orbit*. Each planet has an orbit
of its own, a special path around the sun.

At the same time that the earth is traveling around the
sun, it is also spinning like a top. Each spin takes 24 hours,
or one full day, to complete. When the place where we live
spins around to face the sun, it is daytime. Later, as our side
of the earth spins away from the sun, it becomes nighttime.

The earth is millions of miles away from the sun and the
other planets. But it has a neighbor close by that we call the
moon. The moon is a round ball like the earth, but it is
much smaller. It travels around the earth just as the earth
travels around the sun.

While the earth makes its yearly trip around the sun, the seasons change. This change of seasons happens because the earth tilts toward the sun. When the bottom half of the earth tilts closer to the sun, the top half is farther away. The bottom half then will have summer and the top half will have winter. When our top half of the world has summer weather, it will be winter for people living on the other half of the earth.

259

Learning About Our World

Long ago people thought the earth was flat. They thought if you sailed too far out on the ocean, your ship would fall off the end of the world. And they thought that huge monsters lived in the farthest parts of the ocean.

Most people in those days knew only the land around their hometown or city. But even at that time, some people liked to travel and explore. *Explorers* are people who go to new places to find out about them.

Many explorers traveled over land. They climbed mountains and crossed hot, dry deserts. Other explorers traveled by water. They traveled down rivers in small boats. They sailed out on the seas and oceans in larger ships.

The explorers took maps with them on their travels. A map is a drawing that shows a part of the earth and the places on it. Maps helped the explorers find their way. But many times they went to strange new lands that lay beyond the places on their maps. The explorers wanted to show other people where they had gone, so they drew their own maps of the new lands.

A few explorers sailed far, far out on the ocean—farther than anyone had sailed before. Some people laughed and said, "They will fall off the end of the world, ships and all." But the explorers did not fall off. Instead, they sailed all the way around the earth and came back to where they had started. By doing this, they showed that the earth is round.

When the explorers discovered that the earth is round, they wanted to tell everyone. They wanted maps of the whole round world. That was hard. How can you take a round ball and show all sides of it at once on flat paper?

To draw all of the round earth on flat paper, mapmakers have to squeeze and stretch some parts of it. You can see how they do this in the pictures on the next page.

Flat Maps of a Round World

These pictures show how a mapmaker can make a flat map of something that is round. As you look at the pictures, imagine that you are holding an orange in your hands. Pretend that the orange is the round earth. Peel the orange very carefully, keeping the skin in one piece.

Next, lay the orange peel flat on a piece of paper. There will be some empty places between parts of the peel when it is flat. To fill in those empty places on a map, the mapmakers will have to pull all the pieces together at the edges. You can't do that with an orange peel because it will break. But suppose that the orange peel was actually made of rubber. Then you could carefully stretch all the pieces to join them together at the edges.

In their drawings, the mapmakers can stretch parts of the earth in the same way you can stretch a piece of rubber.

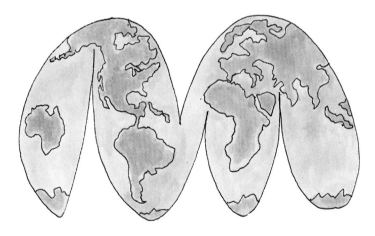

Now turn the page to see a map of our wonderful world.

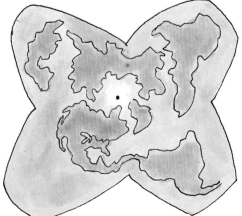

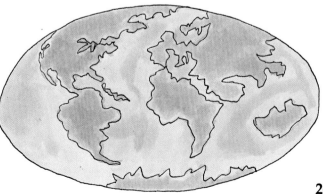

263

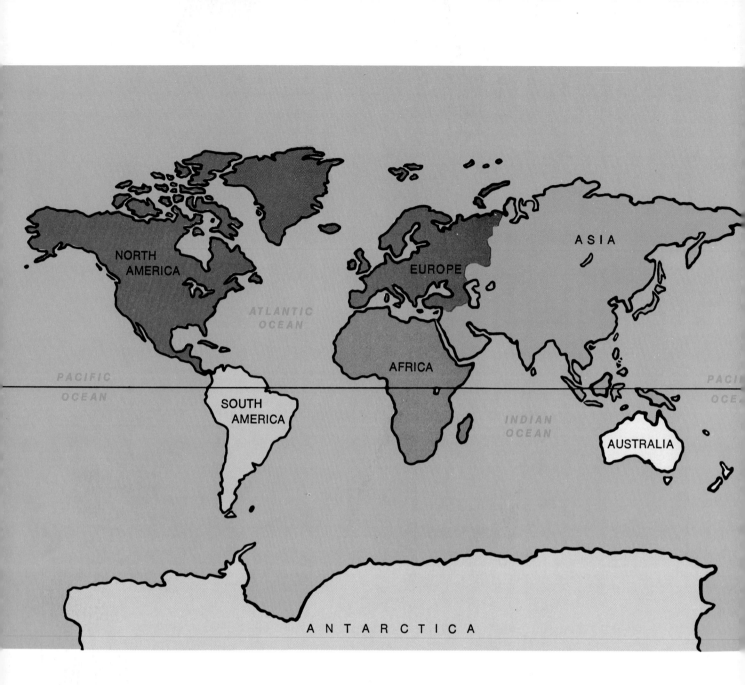

The World

This is a map of the whole world. The blue parts of the map are the oceans. The large areas of land on the map are called *continents*. There are seven continents in the world. Can you count all seven of them? We live on the continent of North America. Can you find it on the map?